Napoleon Bonaparte:
England's Prisoner

NAPOLEON BONAPARTE: ENGLAND'S PRISONER

Frank Giles

CARROLL & GRAF
New York

Carroll & Graf Publishers
An imprint of Avalon Publishing Group, Inc.
161 William Street
16th Floor
New York
NY 10038-2607
www.carrollandgraf.com

First published in the UK by Constable,
an imprint of Constable and Robinson Ltd, 2001

First Carroll & Graf edition 2001

ISBN 0-7867-0906-5

Printed and bound in the EU

For Lily, Max, Joseph,
Lucas and Frederick

Contents

List of Illustrations

Napoleon being rowed to HMS *Bellerophon*, 1815
Bellerophon at Plymouth, with Bonaparte on board, surrounded
    by boatloads of sightseers
Bonaparte on *Bellerophon* from the painting by Sir Charles Eastlake
Napoleon on board *Bellerophon* from a painting by Sir W.Q.
    Orchardson
Bonaparte's dinner table in HMS *Northumberland*
View of Longwood, Bonaparte's place of detention at St Helena
Bonaparte at St Helena, dictating to Gourgaud
An English portrait of Lieut-General Sir Hudson Lowe
A French portrait of Sir Hudson Lowe
Bonaparte in his garden at Longwood
Bonaparte undoing cases of books, many of them sent by Lady
    Holland

Bonaparte 'musing'
The death of Bonaparte, 1821
Lord Holland
Lady Holland
Holland House
Dr O'Meara
The exhumation of Bonaparte, 1840
Bonaparte's funeral cortège in the Place de la Concorde

Dramatis Personae

London: The Prince Regent (later George IV)
Lord Liverpool (Prime Minister)
Lord Castlereagh (Foreign Secretary)
Lord Bathurst (Secretary for War and the Colonies
– the Minister directly responsible for Napoleon's
captivity at St Helena)
Lord and Lady Holland (Bonapartist sympathisers)

St Helena: Napoleon Bonaparte (ex-Emperor of the French)
Sir Hudson Lowe (Governor of St Helena)
General Bertrand (Grand Marshal of the Palace)
Madame Bertrand
General Montholon (A.D.C. to Napoleon)
Madame Montholon
General Gourgaud (Orderly Officer)
Emmanuel Las Cases (Secretary)
Barry O'Meara (Doctor)

Introduction

At the end of the day on May 5, the anniversary of Napoleon's death in 1821, a person standing in the Place de la Concorde and looking up towards the Arc de Triomphe nearly two miles away may observe the sun setting exactly in the middle of the arch – or so it is said. Whether true or not, the fact that such a story should exist indicates the power of the Napoleonic legend.

I myself am not an enthusiastic Napoleonist, indeed not a Napoleonist at all. In my view, despite his superlative talents, his extraordinary career and his real achievements, he did more harm than good to France and to Europe. But many people, from all over the world, would not agree. They would disagree principally, I contend, because of what they have imbibed of the Napoleonic legend: that elaborate and extensive reworking of history to which Napoleon, with unflagging zeal, devoted himself while living out his years of captivity at St Helena.

The message that reached the world, multiplied and magnified by poets and historians, took root, for obvious reasons, most profoundly in France. But it affected other cultures as well, including up to a point our own British view of Napoleon, alive and dead.

In essence, the legend pretended (in the French sense of the word, meaning 'claimed') that if it had not been for the reactionary monarchs of Europe and the envy of England, Napoleon would have emerged as the architect of a federation of free European peoples of which the nucleus and inspiration would have been enlightened and peace-loving France. That this palpably doctored version of events has received such wide credence is a recognition of the immense reputation Napoleon created for himself in not much more than twenty years. Additional elements in the growth of the legend were the pity felt for the prisoner on St Helena; and, for a certain section of English (British) opinion, the well-known national characteristic of siding with the underdog, which Napoleon on his Atlantic outpost had certainly become.

Chateaubriand (no Napoleonist) says in his *Mémoires d'Outre – Tombe*, that 'after [Napoleon's] death, as his sufferings on St Helena became better known, people's hearts began to soften; his tyranny was forgotten ...' It was this passage that set me wondering about those sufferings and Britain's alleged part in causing them.

As this book begins with the events of 1815, it is obviously not another life of Napoleon Bonaparte, to add to the countless biographies already extant. Nor is it a psychological, medical or any other sort of –ical study of a much-studied personality. It is equally not a re-telling, except in a certain context, of the story of the St Helena years. To do that adequately, as others have done before, would require a visit to the island; to my regret, that has not been possible – or at least has not been achieved.

What I have tried to do is to re-examine the question of whether the British government of the day treated its prisoner (a designation to which Napoleon would never admit) in an unjustifiably harsh and inhumane way. What was contemporary or near-contemporary opinion about these matters? For example, as the years wore on, and memories began to fade, did British feelings undergo a change in favour of letting bygones be bygones?

This involved much reading, some of which has proved fruitful. But some of the analysis remains unavoidably speculative. As a former journalist, I know how difficult, not to say impossible, it is to enter into the minds of numbers of people at any particular moment. Today, opinion polls and focus groups try to make audible what the *vox populi* is saying. But they are apt to be unreliable, and anyway they did not exist in 1815.

George Rudé, a social historian and student of crowd behaviour, frankly admits that 'there is a great deal in the motivation of crowds, whether in their "collective mentality" or in that of the individuals that compose them, that defies the historian's or the social scientist's analysis' (*The Face of the Crowd*). Frederic Raphael, writing in *The Spectator* of 25 November 2000 makes another useful point about crowd-reading: 'To seek always to discover what people really think and feel deep down is, often, to accuse them of greater pro-fundity than they possess.'

So the task of anyone seeking to establish what the British 'thought' about Napoleon is a challenging one. Even if some part of it can be satisfactorily accomplished, there can be no uniformity. There is no single view about Napoleon, his role in history and the rights and wrongs of his captivity. As Professor Pieter Geyl puts it in the preface to his fascinating account of the differing approach to Napoleon by eminent French historians (*Napoleon, For and Against*): 'It goes without saying that the various writers who have tried to express their opinions of Napoleon and his career have reached different conclusions.'

A concurrent theme of the book, growing out of the attempt to answer fundamental questions about what really happened at St Helena, is a reassessment of the role and conduct of Sir Hudson Lowe, the Governor of the island and hence the guardian of Napoleon from 1816 until his death in 1821. Lowe has been reviled by historians on both sides of the Channel, and I believe it is possible (and justifiable) to show him, unattractive though in many ways he was, in a much more favourable light. I do not suppose I will win over the critics, but at least I find myself in the good company of the first Duke of Wellington who, despite a highly negative view of Lowe as Napoleon's gaoler, in the end argued that he had received very shabby treatment.

Readers may wonder at the use I have made of the terms 'Napoleonist' and 'Bonapartist'. Orthodox historical definition suggests they are not the same. To be a Napoleonist should mean someone with (often boundless) veneration for and sympathy with Napoleon as a man and leader of men. Bonapartism, on the other hand, has come in general to mean a personal and authoritarian method of governing which is specially associated with France. It is a recurrent theme in nineteenth century French history. Apart from the first Emperor himself, no one was more Bonapartist than his nephew, Napoleon III, in the way in which he achieved and kept power. General Boulanger, the swashbuckling adventurer in the early days of the Third Republic, was an embryo Bonapartist, even if he supported royalist claims to the throne. More than eighty years later, General de Gaulle, returning to power after years of self-imposed political exile, was suspected (wrongly) of harbouring Bonapartist intentions.

For better or for worse I have used the two terms interchangeably. In this book, to be a Napoleonist is also to be a Bonapartist: someone who regards the fallen Emperor, indeed his whole career from its beginning, with admiration, mingled, once the St Helena episode had begun, with pity. The admiration was not always total: even the warmest of English fans found the execution of the Duc d'Enghien hard to swallow. But in general the English Napoleonists/Bonapartists, though not numerous, were united in thinking that Bonaparte was a great man and that Britain had and has much to answer for in her treatment of him.

With two important exceptions, I have used secondary sources in telling the story. A selective bibliography will be found at the end of the book. 'Selective' it has to be. The literature is enormous, and I am sure I have missed or remained ignorant of many important pieces of evidence. In particular, the literary references in Chapter 5 are obviously capable of expansion and development.

The two exceptions are firstly the Royal Archives and secondly the Hudson Lowe papers. I am grateful to HM the Queen for her permission to quote from the Archives, and to Mr Oliver Everett, the Librarian at Windsor Castle, for his courteous and prompt answers to questions.

The Lowe papers are housed in the British Library, to whose helpful assistants I pay a warm tribute. The reference numbers are: ADD MSS 20107–20133 (Lowe's official papers) of which 20115–20133 relate to St Helena. 20135–20161 and 20199–20240 also have to do with St Helena and other matters pertaining. Bound in (mostly) folio volumes, the relevant ones contain handwritten originals, or handwritten copies of letters between Lord Bathurst (the responsible Minister in London) and Lowe, despatches, memoranda, and other documents concerning Napoleon's captivity and related matters. They are remarkably complete. As Lowe himself pointed out, 'There are perhaps few if any public administrations of any kind, of which the records are so full and complete as those of my government at St Helena'. The remark suggests either a paragon of method and orderliness or a bureaucrat festooned in red tape: perhaps both.

These papers were used exhaustively by William Forsyth when he came to write the three-volume *History of the captivity of Napoleon at St Helena* (1853). It is a prolonged and on the whole successful attempt to defend Lowe against the accusations made about him. Some writers allege that Forsyth was not impartial, making selective use of the material and suppressing certain evidence. My trawl through the papers did not at first glance seem to sustain these charges, but this is not to deny that Forsyth, like all apologists, was bent upon presenting his subject in the best possible light.

I am grateful to Mr Charles Hargrove in Paris for following up some queries there. Also to Mr Hugh Cobbe and Dr Christopher Wright, of the Manuscript Department of the British Library for kindly supplying some details about the portraits of Sir Hudson Lowe. Mr Alan Bell, Librarian of the London Library, and Miss Alethea Hayter, were very helpful in tracking down the Haydon painting of Napoleon 'musing' at St Helena (see book plate section). The index is the work of the prince of his craft, Mr Douglas Matthews, formerly Librarian of the London Library.

My special thanks are due to Lord Briggs (Asa Briggs) former Vice-Chancellor of Sussex University and former Provost of Worcester College Oxford, and to Professor Douglas Johnson, Professor of French History, University College London, 1968–90. Both read the entire typescript and made detailed comments thereon. For these distinguished historians to devote so much of their time and expertise was a source of great encouragement. Their advice was invaluable, but I remain solely responsible for everything that appears between these covers.

Finally, I thank most warmly my publisher, Ben Glazebrook, of Constable Publishers, for all his help, advice and friendship. To be on good relations with one's publisher is a useful, indeed near-essential accompaniment to the act of authorship; such has certainly been the case with this book.

Sarah Smith, the desk editor at Constable has excelled in efficiency and helpfulness and I owe her a debt of gratitude.

1

'... The Hospitality of the British People'

In Paris, on the morning of 22 June 1815, four days after the Battle of Waterloo, the Emperor Napoleon abdicated (for the second time within fifteen months). His declaration 'to the French people' followed an ultimatum from the Upper and Lower Chambers (the Peers and the Representatives) that if he did not step down they would depose him. After the military reverses, the sudden return to Paris, the shock and humiliation of defeat, this was for Napoleon the final blow. For a few hours the stricken but still-defiant Emperor had played with the idea of dissolving the Chambers, assuming the powers of a temporary dictator, and rallying national resistance to the invading allied armies. Some of his entourage, notably his brother Lucien, urged just such a course. But he hesitated, and then it was too late. 'My political life is over,' he had said in his declaration, 'and I proclaim my son Emperor of the French, under the title of Napoleon II.'

The Chambers showed little inclination to approve this proclamation. Despite Napoleon's contention that he had only abdicated in favour of his son, and that if this were not enacted he would withdraw the abdication, the Chambers decided to establish a provisional government, instead of the council of regency desired by Napoleon. The Executive Commission charged with carrying on this government then published a decree according to which, as Napoleon II had not been recognised as sovereign by any power, it was declared to be the duty of the Commission to act provisionally in the name of the French people in treating with the victorious allies. So the Napoleonic dynasty went into abeyance until such time as the Emperor's nephew, Louis, succeeded in reviving the Imperial title in 1852.

Twenty-one days later, on 13 July, from a French frigate lying off Rochefort, where he had toyed with various audacious plans for seeking refuge in the United States, Napoleon dictated his famous letter[1] to the Prince Regent. Carefully avoiding any hint of surrender, still less any acceptance of responsibility for the defeat of France, he said he came 'like Themistocles to throw myself upon the hospitality of the British people – I put myself under the protection of their laws, which I claim from Your Royal Highness, as the most powerful, the most constant, and the most generous of my enemies'.

This decision to give himself up to the British was only arrived at after prolonged (and uncharacteristic) dithering and procrastination. His stepdaughter Hortense, Queen of Holland and daughter of the Empress Josephine, had suggested to him, while he was still at the Elysée in Paris, that he should ask the Tsar Alexander for asylum, or alternatively should seek the protection of his own father-in-law, the Austrian Emperor. Neither of these ideas appealed to Napoleon. If he gave himself up to Alexander, he reasoned, he would be surrendering to a man, whereas if he chose England he would at least be surrendering to a nation.[2] Hortense did not agree. 'They would shut you up in the Tower of London,' she said.[3] The Hapsburg connection was even less attractive to the defeated Emperor. Had not the Emperor Francis kept Marie-Louise and the King of Rome, his wife and child, from him? But even the possible advantages of placing himself in the hands of the English might have its drawbacks. 'My life there would be ridiculous and uneasy too. Even if I kept quiet they wouldn't believe it. Every fog [like most Frenchmen to this day,

2

Napoleon evidently considered that England was permanently wreathed in fog] would be suspected of tempting me to the coast. . .'[4]

Then came the idea of America. Napoleon apparently thought that he would be welcome in a country that had been at war with England from 1812 to 1814. His brother Joseph, the former King of Spain, had already determined to go there. Carnot, the brilliant engineer and member of the original revolutionary Committee of Public Safety, who advised him not to go to England, further encouraged Napoleon. 'They hate you too much, you would be insulted by prize-fighters. Don't hesitate to go to America. From there, you can still make your enemies tremble. If France is to fall under the yoke of the Bourbons again, your presence in a free country will be a support to national opinion.'[5] So the ex-Emperor asked the provisional government in Paris to provide him with passports and the use of two frigates, then lying off Rochefort.

After some delay, during which Napoleon left Paris for Malmaison, Fouché, the former Minister of Police and now the effective head of the provisional government (Napoleon believed him, not without reason, to be 'a scoundrel of the deepest dye'), gave instructions for the frigates to be made available. But for the voyage to America to be possible, British agreement was needed. The Royal Navy was watching the French coast. As he waited at Malmaison, Napoleon grasped at straws. Wellington's and Blücher's armies were closing in on Paris, and Napoleon proposed to the provisional government that with the status of General, not Emperor, he should reassume command of what was left of the army, drive the enemy back and thus provide the government with more favourable a stance from which to negotiate with the allies. Having achieved this, he would then depart for the New World. Fouché and his colleagues, for whom Napoleon's presence was becoming an embarrassment, rejected this plan and instead advised him to leave forthwith for Rochefort; otherwise he risked being captured by the allies.

Napoleon regretfully complied and, on the morning of 2 July, reached Rochefort, to be greeted by an enthusiastic crowd. There was still no word of French passports or British safe-conduct. Nevertheless it is arguable at this stage that had he been prepared to take the risk, he could have slipped through the British blockade, gained the open sea and set sail for America. The so-called blockade, in those early days of July, was maintained only by the Royal Naval brig *Myrmidon* and the old frigate *Bellerophon* (known to British sailors as *Billy Ruffian*). The *Saale*, one of the French frigates, was among the newest and swiftest of the French fleet. Had he made a run for it, the government in Paris would have been in no position to stop him, even assuming it had wanted to. Provided it could have satisfied the conquering allies that it had not aided or abetted the escape, Napoleon's flight could have solved an increasingly burdensome problem.

But the ex-Emperor had not only his own safety to think about but that of his suite, consisting of about sixty people, including wives and children. He could have fallen in with another plan, though it would have had the same objections, which was to take passage in a Danish sloop, commanded by a Frenchman, where he would have concealed himself, in the case of British interception, in a padded barrel fitted with breathing tubes. 'The Emperor felt it undignified,' wrote Marchand, his valet, 'to be hiding in the hold of the ship if he should be captured.'[6] It would have been almost equally undignified, as well as risky, to have accepted the invitation of six enterprising young naval officers to break the British blockade in their *chassemarée*, or decked whaleboat. It is less easy to understand why Napoleon turned down a surely more acceptable alternative, to embark in a French corvette lying to the south, in the mouth of the Gironde, whose captain was eager to make the attempt.

By this time (8 July) Napoleon and most of his suite had boarded the *Saale* in response to orders from the provisional government in Paris. Fresh advice came only a day later that he should either sail immediately or go aboard one of the British ships. Faced with this peremptory reminder that he no longer had any role to play in the destinies of France, Napoleon made the first moves towards sounding out British reactions. From the *Saale* he sent two of his staff, General Savary, Duke of Rovigo, and Count de Las Cases, to see Captain Maitland, the captain of *Bellerophon.*

What was in his mind as he made these initial overtures can only be guesswork, though there are certain indications. Compared with giving himself up to the Bourbons, the Prussians or the Austrians – Blücher had already sworn to have him hanged – surrender to England must have been a more promising alternative. As later pages of this book will reveal, he had a certain admiration for British institutions. Moreover, he had already, in 1814, during the negotiations leading up to his first abdication, expressed an interest in seeking asylum in England. Castlereagh, the British Foreign Secretary, gave him no encouragement. The wife of Count Bertrand, who as Grand Marshal was head of the Imperial household, was the daughter of an Irishman and had spent much of her childhood in England. Although Marchand, the valet, records[7] that Fanny Bertrand's views weighed not at all with Napoleon, he says also that she had no doubts about his being received there with due ceremony.

The most simple explanation is often the best, so it seems perfectly credible that Napoleon, as he prepared these first steps towards what he intended should be an honourable exile in England, had genuinely convinced himself that what he wanted he would get. He could also have harboured the thought – as his career showed, his was the kind of ambition that never rested – of using England as a possible springboard for further political and military adventures. In any case, he dictated a letter for his two emissaries to take to Maitland. It consisted of no more than a request for information about the passports 'which had been promised to him', to enable him to proceed to America. This was a trick. Napoleon could not fail to have known that no passports had been promised.

Maitland, having read the letter, replied that he was in no position to say what the British government's intentions might be, but that as France and Britain were still at war he could not allow any warship to sail out of Rochefort. Maitland had by now received instructions from his flag officer, Admiral Sir Henry Hotham, to prevent Napoleon from escaping by intercepting him and transferring him to *Bellerophon*. He was under no obligation to disclose his orders to the representatives of what was still an enemy power. But in his conversation with the two Frenchmen (which seems to have been politely correct), Maitland rather unwisely (in view of subsequent controversy) went further. In answer to his visitors' assurances (for what they were worth) that Napoleon's political ambitions were at an end and that he intended 'retiring into obscurity', Maitland said, 'if that is the case, why not seek an asylum in England?' They replied – with what sincerity it is impossible to know – by listing the reasons why Napoleon did not wish to choose England, including the fact that 'he has been accustomed to consider the English as his most inveterate enemies, and they have been induced to look upon him as a monster'.

Both Maitland[8] and Las Cases[9] later wrote their own accounts of what had passed between them, and almost inevitably the two records differ. French historians with Bonapartist sympathies insist that the British, by false promises of favourable treatment, lured the ex-Emperor into surrendering. Napoleon himself, dismayed later by the prospect of St Helena, levelled this same charge, claiming that he had been the victim of a trap. There were subsequent meetings in *Bellerophon* off Rochefort, at one of which Maitland took the opportunity of repeating that he 'could not stipulate as to the reception of Bonaparte in England, but that he, Bonaparte, must consider himself at the disposal of His Royal Highness, the Prince Regent'. According to Maitland's account, Las Cases replied that he was aware of these reservations and had so informed Napoleon. Las Cases makes no mention of this point in his voluminous *Mémoriale*, published after Napoleon's death.

Early on the morning of 15 July, Napoleon, wearing the uniform of a colonel of the Chasseurs of the Guard, with the famous olive-coloured greatcoat over it, came aboard *Bellerophon*. To Maitland, who was waiting to receive him with full honours, he said: 'I am come to throw myself on the protection of your Prince and laws' – words that, coming from someone with whom Britain had been at war for almost twenty-two years, combined sheer cheek with a certain audacious dignity. His embarkation in the ship and his subsequent passage to England meant that he came daily into contact with ordinary British people, in the shape of the officers and men of the ship's company. They were somewhat different from the class and standing of the British of whom he had previous experience. After the conclusion of the Peace of Amiens in March 1802, Paris had been full of English visitors, 5,000 of them, according to Andrew Merry, the acting British Ambassador. Some were simply curious, some, of artistic tendencies, wanted to see the collections in the Louvre (much enriched by the spoils of war from Napoleon's Italian campaign) and some simply wanted to renew earlier French friendships. There was indeed some bewilderment, poetically expressed by Wordsworth, about what had drawn all these visitors to Paris: 'is it a reed that's shaken by the wind/or what is it that ye go forth to see?'

Whatever it was, the more prominent among them either tried to meet, or succeeded in meeting, Bonaparte, then First Consul. These included various members of the Foxite Whigs, notably Lord and Lady Holland, ardent Bonapartists, and the former's uncle, Charles James Fox. As a leading Whig, Francophile and opponent of the war with France, Fox was suspected by many of being such a Bonapartist as to come under the suspicion of treason. It is true that in the period leading up to the Peace of Amiens he saw and approved of Bonaparte as a peacemaker – 'moderate, wise and pacific'.[10] But before this he had been highly critical, finding the coup d'état of Brumaire 'a very bad beginning – the manner of the thing was quite odious'.[11] When the Revolution burst on the world in 1789, with a rather superficial tendency to think that British political history could be compared with apparently similar events in France, he described its leaders as the French descendants of the Whigs in 1688. But when the Revolution turned into Terror, Fox was outraged, writing of Robespierre as a 'miserable miscreant'.

Bonaparte had first offered peace terms in 1800, a move that not only won Fox's approval, coming as they did from 'this extraordinary man', but also caused him to execrate Pitt's government's rejection of them. In his Francophilia and thirst for peace, Fox was prepared to minimalise or ignore the various aspects of Bonaparte's rule that could not possibly be considered constitutional or liberal. When peace eventually came in 1802, Fox was delighted: 'it is an excellent thing, and I do not like it the worse for its being so very triumphant a peace for France.'[12] Not surprisingly, these sentiments did not endear him to British public opinion. In France, on the other hand, he enjoyed great esteem and popularity, to the point that the British Embassy indignantly considered that Fox was flattering the French and running down his own country. In fact, he himself showed no great urge to meet the First Consul, and when they did come face to face the encounter was by no means a meeting of minds.

Bonaparte began by greeting him effusively as 'the greatest man of one of the greatest countries in the world'.[13] He had evidently prepared his speech and was anxious to impress his visitor. This he largely failed to do if Lady Bessborough, a witness to the affair, is to be believed. According to her, Fox took exception, in vigorous terms, to Bonaparte's arguments for maintaining a strong standing army; Bonaparte himself was 'startled, surprised and displeased' by this reaction.[14]

The next day, Fox was invited to the First Consul's dinner, together with Lord Holland, his nephew. Again the fur flew. Bonaparte complained about the excessive liberty enjoyed by the English press, especially in its comments about himself. Fox retorted that freedom of the press was a necessary evil. The two men also disagreed, at a later meeting, about the difficulties (as Bonaparte saw them) of abolishing the slave trade. Fox's entry in his diary about the dinner was prosaic, almost dismissive: 'near 200 people, very magnif. [sic]. Was presented to Mme. [i.e. Josephine]. Liked her very much.'

On the whole, Fox came away from Paris a disillusioned man. For all his Francophilia, he had found the Bonapartist system, with its protocol and pomp, to be 'a court'.[15] He spoke 'very lightly of the abilities of Bonaparte – very deficient upon every subject, no powers or extent of mind – the predominance of Bonaparte [is] the greatest imposition that was ever practised upon the whole world'. Such scepticism about Bonaparte did not save Fox from public criticism. Coleridge accused him of becoming the 'temporary courtier of Bonaparte', and Cobbett, in his *Political Register*, asserted that he was trying to use the First Consul to help him, Fox, back to office in London.

Though Fox remained until his death in 1806 opposed to the war with France, as he was to any idea that Britain should try to help the Bourbons regain their throne, he was not, as the quotations already given suggest, a confirmed or fanatical Bonapartist. He would almost certainly have opposed Napoleon's banishment to St Helena on the grounds of justice and humanity; but it is perhaps significant that his nephew, Lord Holland, who was to become vehement about the treatment of the ex-Emperor, was equally disenchanted by his contact with the First Consul in 1802. He described him as 'undoubtedly impatient of contradiction, to a degree amounting not only to a blemish in his moral character, but to weakness in his understanding'.[16]

Among others in Paris in that year of peace was the Duke of Bedford, one of the grandest of the Whig grandees, who considered Napoleon 'a most extraordinary man', Hazlitt, future author of a weighty and adulatory *Life* of Napoleon, the poet Samuel Rogers, the barrister and law reformer Sir Samuel

Romilly, both of them members of the Holland House set, and a young naval officer named Maitland. According to the *Moniteur*, the official government paper, the last was received in audience by the First Consul, though judging from the reminiscences they both left behind them neither seems to have any recollection of the occasion when twelve years later they met again in dramatically different circumstances.

Whatever the British may have thought about Napoleon – and opinions were sharply divided, as this book seeks to show – he himself sometimes expressed admiration of British institutions and characteristics. During his first exile on Elba, where he retained the Imperial title, even though the empire over which he ruled had been reduced to one small island, he gave audiences to curious English visitors, including several Members of Parliament. Among them was a cousin of Lord Holland, George Vernon (who later took the name of Harcourt, on succeeding to the Nuneham estates near Oxford), and Mr Fazakerley. This conversation lasted for four hours, Napoleon, as usual, doing most of the talking. Throughout this time, the three men remained standing. According to the record which the Englishmen later compiled,[17] the Emperor admired the 'aristocratic' system of government in England: 'your aristocracy controls Parliament and can sway opinion . . . in France our 'tail' is good, our 'head' bad, in England your head is good, your tail bad . . . England is never so great as she is today – but her day will come, she will fall like all great empires.' The two visitors, through deference or conviction or both, praised what Napoleon had done for Paris and for communications via the Simplon to the south. But they seemed from their own account to have abstained from further comment: their interest was to let Napoleon do the talking.

During the Elba interlude (May 1814 – April 1815), Napoleon also received Lord Ebrington (later the second Earl Fortescue), Lord John Russell (later Earl Russell and Prime Minister, Bertrand Russell's grandfather), Mr Douglas and Mr MacNamara. All these were MPs and all, except Douglas, Whigs, as were Vernon and Fazakerley. They all left records, Russell composing his decades later; none was so extensive as Ebrington's.[18] He had two sessions with the Emperor, lasting in all seven and a half hours. Once again, Napoleon did most of the talking, although Ebrington did ask him some critical questions about the execution of the Duc d'Enghien. That apart, Napoleon dwelt on some of the points he had made to Vernon: admiration for the House of Lords, curiosity about the English administration of justice, and queries about how he would be treated were he to retire to England (Ebrington said that violent feelings against him were 'daily subsiding' now that the war was over). Napoleon also asked after some of the English he had met in Paris in 1802: the Duke and Duchess of Bedford, Lord Holland and 'a good deal about Mr Fox'.

He omitted to ask after Lord Whitworth, who was briefly British Ambassador in Paris after the signature of the Peace of Amiens. The omission is hardly surprising. In March 1803 the two men, First Consul and Ambassador, had a stand-up row in public – except that it takes two to make a row and in this case there was only one rowdy. The episode has gone down in the history of diplomacy as an example of how not to conduct affairs of state.

Under the Treaty of Amiens, Britain was required to cede the island of Malta to France. Various signs and suspicions that Bonaparte was contemplating expansion eastwards, to Egypt and beyond, perhaps to India, aroused misgivings in London. This seemed an unpropitious time to be giving up Malta, with its famous harbour and fortifications, which could be so important in impeding French designs. Bonaparte, of course, did not see it like that. At a diplomatic reception at the Tuileries on 13 March 1803, he shouted at Whitworth, in a way that the assembled company could not fail to hear and see, *'Malheur à ceux qui ne respectent pas les traités. Ils en seront responsable à toute Europe'*. Whitworth reported to London that the First

Consul 'was too agitated to prolong the conversation. I therefore made no answer, and he retired to his apartments repeating the last phrase. Two hundred people heard this conversation (if such it can be called) and I am persuaded that there was not a single person who did not feel the extreme impropriety and total want of dignity as well as of decency on the occasion.'

The Dictionary of National Biography, from which this account is drawn, says that Whitworth's demeanour throughout the event 'was generally marked by a dignity and *impassibilité* worthy of the best traditions of aristocratic diplomacy'. Bonaparte later challenged the accepted version of what had passed. In captivity at St Helena, while describing the Ambassador as '*habile*' and '*adroit*', he said that his account was full of mistakes. Given Napoleon's life-long tendency to fall into rages when crossed, it seems much more likely that Whitworth's report is well founded. It certainly appeared that Britain was in breach of the treaty. If so, Napoleon's accusations if not his manners were justified. But London had the support of both Russia and Turkey, both apprehensive of France's territorial ambitions; in international politics, national interests sometimes have to override formal obligations.

Even allowing for Ebrington's desire to be agreeable to his Imperial host, his generalisation about British opinion must be open to question. That opinion had ebbed and flowed, like the tides, as the Napoleonic era developed. Sometimes Napoleon's military prowess commanded admiration – as, for example, when Canning, in a speech on the army estimates in December 1802, confessed to being unable 'to shut my eyes to the superiority of his talents . . . it is his genius, his character, that keeps the world in awe'. But the execution of the Duc d'Enghien in 1804 brought execration from both Tories and Whigs, while the Imperial coronation, involving Bonaparte's self-proclamation as Emperor, evoked feelings of amusement and contempt that 'the Corsican attorney's son' (*The Times*) should presume thus to elevate himself. (The Duke of

Wellington was later, in his robust way, to declare that Napoleon was 'no gentleman'.) His Spanish adventure was widely condemned; even the staunchly Whig *Edinburgh Review* called it an 'outrageous usurpation'. By 1814 dislike and distrust of Napoleon was at its height. To probably the majority of English people, Napoleon's downfall appeared to represent the triumph of good over evil.[19]

Thackeray, in *Vanity Fair*, makes his shrewish anti-heroine, the French-speaking Becky Sharp, shout '*Vive la France, Vive l'Empereur, Vive Bonaparte*', as she leaves Miss Pinkerton's Academy, in about the year 1812. But her attitude cannot be considered representative. A permanent member of the awkward squad, Becky can always be counted on to voice some disaffected or outrageous sentiment. Similarly, the reaction of the book's saccharine heroine, Amelia Osborne, to Napoleon's first abdication in 1814 – she clapped her hands and said prayers – had nothing to do with Bonapartism or its converse. She was simply overjoyed that the war (as she and most other people thought) was over, so that her worthless but adored fiancé George Osborne would not have to risk injury or death by exposing himself to French bayonets or swords. The following year, he was killed at Waterloo.

The Holland House set, of course, stood conspicuously apart from these general trends, none more so than the frenetic Lady Holland, who had been presented to the First Consul in Paris in 1802. In Florence in 1814 she sent some parcels of newspapers to the Emperor in Elba, having wheedled permission to do so out of Colonel Neil Campbell, the chief allied representative on Elba. It was from these papers that Napoleon first read of the possibility that he might be moved from Elba and incarcerated elsewhere, perhaps St Helena. This may have set him planning on an escape, for according to Campbell, who saw him soon after the delivery of Lady Holland's newspapers, he said he would not consent to being transported from Elba and would resist any attempt to do so by force. Given the degree of Lady

Holland's admiration, it is surprising that she did not join the flow of English visitors to Elba and the Imperial villa there; instead, she and her husband went off to Rome to stay with Napoleon's brother Lucien, who had abdicated from the throne of Holland in 1810 and lived ever since in Rome under the name of the Comte de St Leu.

In contrast to these previous contacts with and memories of a group of more or less sympathetic, more or less grandee specimens of the British race, Napoleon's journey to England in *Bellerophon* brought him in touch with a more modest range of British manhood. He already had some personal knowledge of the Royal Navy. In May 1814 HMS *Undaunted*, under the command of Captain Usher, RN, had conveyed the Emperor and his suite to Elba. He was received on board with a royal salute and manned yards, a courtesy for which Usher was subsequently criticised in England (unjustly, because Napoleon was entitled to such honours). According to a French source,[20] he made a favourable impression on all the ship's officers, while the lower deck, expecting an arch fiend, were 'greatly surprised by the exhibition of so much kindness of manners'. One old salt, Joe Hinton, the bo'sun, refused to be converted. 'Humbug,' he muttered whenever he heard his shipmates praising Napoleon; and when the Emperor arrived at Elba and handed out 200 Napoleons to be distributed among the ship's company, all that Hinton could find to say, in the way of thanks, was 'wish your Honour good health and better luck next time'.

One of the more bizarre events of the Elba interregnum, once more bringing Napoleon into contact with the Royal Navy, was when he attended a reception on board *Undaunted* in honour of George III's birthday (4 June 1814). An eyewitness recounted how the ship's company gave the Emperor 'three rousing cheers'. The entire crew seemed pleased to see him. At some point during the party Napoleon said that 'if I went to England, the English government would be afraid of my popularity and would pack me off'. When he left the ship, there were renewed cheers.

The welcome accorded to the defeated Emperor by *Bellerophon* once more revealed Napoleon's sure touch with fighting men. Indeed, so courteous was the reception that, together with the honours later paid him on board the flagship of Maitland's admiral, it is hardly surprising if Napoleon took at face value Las Cases' assurance that on the warship they would all be on British soil, enjoying the sacred laws of hospitality and the benefit of the civil laws of England. 'They are a great nation, noble and generous; they will treat me as I ought to be treated,' Napoleon rashly prophesied.[21]

Vivid accounts of his arrival in *Bellerophon* have been left by Maitland and by one of the ship's midshipmen, George Home. From these it is clear that the Emperor (ex-Emperor, according to British usage) cast a powerful spell over the sailors. 'And now,' wrote Home in his memoirs,[22] published many years later – despite or because of his youth, he became a fanatical Bonapartist the moment he saw Napoleon coming up the gangway – 'and now came the great little man himself, wrapped up in his grey overcoat buttoned to the chin. . .' During the following days Napoleon conducted himself, as Maitland wrote, 'as a Royal personage . . . which under the circumstances I considered it would have been both ungracious and uncalled for in me to have disputed'. This goes far to explain subsequent misunderstanding and French accusations of British perfidy. Whatever Napoleon's innermost feelings, he chose to behave (acted?) as though his Imperial status was unchanged. The navy responded by putting on its traditional display of protocol and hospitality (a tradition still generally observed today in Royal Naval ships and shore stations) for the benefit of Napoleon and his companions, who included Lieutenant-General Bertrand and Brigadier-General Montholon, the two most senior courtiers and their wives.

Bonapartist historians make much of the fact that while Maitland and his superior, Admiral Hotham, were treating

15

Napoleon with semi-regal status, both officers were under the Admiralty's secret orders to keep him, once they had him in their hands, 'in careful custody', and to convey him to the nearest port in England as soon as possible. There was in fact nothing incompatible between these orders and their respectful attitude towards the fallen Emperor. The account of the dinner-party on Napoleon's first night on *Bellerophon* does make some curious reading none the less. No defeated foe in the two great wars of the twentieth century was ever treated thus.

Hitler was dead by his own hand when the Second World War ended (in the West) in 1945. At the end of the First, Kaiser Wilhelm II did not surrender but abdicated and fled to neutral Holland two days before the 1918 Armistice. He was regarded by many, in Britain and elsewhere, as a war criminal – 'Hang the Kaiser', etc. But though the victorious allies in 1919 did consider that he and his accomplices should be brought before an international court, nothing came of it, and he was left in peace to live out his dreary life at Doorn until his death in 1941.

Admiral Hotham had arrived in his flagship, HMS *Superb*, earlier in the day, and in the afternoon came on board *Bellerophon* to call on Bonaparte. Dinner followed, prepared by the Imperial chefs and served on Imperial silver. Napoleon led the way into the dining cabin and seated himself in the principal place, with the Admiral on his right and Madame Bertrand on his left. Then the prisoner (or honoured guest, according to individual interpretation) retired for the night, after Marchand, the valet, had demonstrated the clever mechanism of his master's camp bed. The bewitched Home wrote in his diary: 'when Admiral Hotham and the officers uncovered in the presence of Napoleon, they treated him with the respect due to the man himself, to his innate greatness, which did not lie in the crown of France or the iron crown of Italy, but in the actual superiority of the man and the rest of his species'.

Clearly, the personal effect that Napoleon created, even in this moment of defeat and surrender, comes into the equation.

However much the English people had been conditioned to regard him (with reason) as their greatest enemy, as the bogey-man whose thirst for conquest and reputation for cruelty was then and well into the next century invoked by British nannies ('Boney'll get you') against their recalcitrant charges, his own peculiar charm, as well as his reputation as a superman, could not, and did not, fail to impress itself on these uncynical, straightforward sailors.

Maitland summed it up very well when he wrote:

> his manners were extremely pleasing and affable, he joined in every conversation, relating numerous anecdotes, and en-deavoured in every way to promote good humour – he possessed, to a wonderful degree, a facility in making a favour-able impression – he appeared to have great command of temper, for though no man could have had greater trials than fell to his lot, during the time he remained on board *Bellerophon*, he never, in my presence, or as far as I know, allowed a fretful or captious expression to escape him.[23]

Later on, when told of the decision to send him to St Helena, Napoleon revealed a very different disposition, protesting volubly and violently. Could the earlier charm offensive have been an act, designed to ingratiate himself with his English guardians, and thus, so he could have calculated, pave the way to a favourable reception in England? The thought occurred to Maitland, who wrote that even if such were the case, only a great command of temper could have sustained such a perfor-mance.

What this eloquent passage from Maitland's memoirs does not explain was how Napoleon, while telling stories and generally being the life and soul of the party, managed to make himself understood. Few if any of the crew of *Bellerophon* would have been able to speak or understand French, and certainly not Napoleon's French, with its heavy Corsican accent. Even

Maitland, by his own confession, was not proficient in the language, and Napoleon, despite attempts to learn English while at St Helena, never made any progress and soon gave up the struggle. None of the contemporary accounts of conversations between Napoleon and his English interlocutors clarify this point. Holland and his wife talked fluent French as did Charles James Fox, with a good accent. The only members of Napoleon's suite who were fluent in English were Fanny Bertrand and Las Cases, who had lived for several years in England. The same mystery attaches to the many meetings Napoleon had, once *Bellerophon* reached England, with senior naval officers and government representatives, few of whom were proficient French-speakers.

Presumably, Bonaparte would not have been so vivacious during *Bellerophon's* passage had he known of the fate of the Themistocles letter. Before the departure from Rochefort, this had been entrusted to another member of the suite, General Gourgaud. He had gone ahead in HMS *Slaney*, a frigate that had joined the blockade, apparently in the belief that once that ship reached port he would be able to go to London, seek an audience with the Prince Regent and deliver the letter. Gourgaud was a vain and rather foolish man, but he had his Emperor's authority and confidence. His instructions from the latter included a note stating that he, Napoleon, if he could not get to America, wished to settle in England, where he would take the name of Colonel Muiron (an aide-de-camp killed at the Battle of Arcola). 'I wish to live in a country house ten or twelve leagues from London', the note went on, and it would have to be big enough to house all the suite.

Alas for such modest hopes. Maitland says that he made it clear, before Gourgaud set out in *Slaney*, that he would not be allowed to land until permission had been received from London, or sanctioned by the admiral at the port of arrival. And this is what happened. Gourgaud was not allowed, once *Slaney* reached Plymouth, to land and was ordered back to *Bellerophon* once she arrived. A copy of the Themistocles letter did go to London, the messenger being the captain of the *Slaney*. Of all this the French party on *Bellerophon* knew nothing until the ship arrived at Torbay. So they sailed on, ignorant of their true fate, weaving fantasies, Napoleon talking and joking, patting Maitland on the head in avuncular style, attending a theatrical performance got up by the midshipmen.

It was not only middle or junior-rank officers and men who were impressed with the personality and bearing of Napoleon. Someone of much more exalted status was, at least to begin with, similarly affected: Admiral Lord Keith, Commander-in-Chief of the Channel Fleet, flying his flag at Plymouth. He had several encounters with the ex-Emperor on *Bellerophon*, as a result of which he told Maitland: 'damn the fellow, if he had obtained an interview with His Royal Highness [the Prince Regent] in half an hour they would have been the best friends in England.' This remark is complemented by that attributed to the Prince Regent when acquainted with the contents of the Themistocles letter: he said that the mode of addressing him – '*Altesse Royale*' – was quite correct and proper, 'more correct, I must say, than any ever received from Louis XVIII', who had been living in exile in England and who used the form '*Monseigneur*'. That at least is the story that Lord Holland (in his *Foreign Reminiscences*) recounts. But documents in the Royal Archives at Windsor show that in fact Louis XVIII's letters to the Regent did refer to him as '*Votre Altesse Royale*'. So a more likely explanation of the Regent's allegedly favourable reaction to Napoleon's letter is to be found in Napoleon's description of that inordinately vain Prince as 'the most powerful, the most constant and the most generous of my enemies'.

If respect and admiration for the would-be conqueror of Europe characterised the attitude of the Royal Navy, the popular reaction once *Bellerophon* had dropped anchor at Torbay was one of burning curiosity. The warship was immediately surrounded by a number of small boats crammed with people intent on seeing 'this extraordinary man' (Maitland's words). Napoleon's response was that of a man never averse to adulation: he showed himself on deck, at the gangway and at the stern windows of the main cabin, taking off his hat and bowing. The crowds in the boats shouted 'Bonaparte, Bonaparte!' and the more they shouted the more he went through his performance. 'What curious people these English are' he remarked to Maitland; and they continued to be curious in ever-increasing numbers.

A citizen of Brixham described the spectacle thus:

> Boats! There never was before or since such an assembly of craft in Torbay – Torquay was little but a fishermen's village – but the population, such as it was, seemed to have turned out altogether and crossed the bay. From Exmouth, Teignmouth, Plymouth, the boats and yachts continued to arrive all day – and on that day all the country seemed to come in. Gentlemen and ladies on horseback and in carriages; other people in carts and wagons; and to judge by the number of people, all the world inland was flocking to see Bonaparte. The Brixham boatmen had a busy time of it, and must have taken more money in two days than in an ordinary month. It seemed a gala day as the boats thronged round the *Bellerophon*, and Tuesday found Brixham in a whirl of excitement. Every inn was full; and there was not room for the visitors nor stabling for the horses.[24]

Midshipman Home, when he went ashore the morning after arriving at Torbay, was set upon by a group of young ladies who plied him with questions about Bonaparte. They gave him tea and cakes, and he repaid their hospitality by assuring them that if they once saw Bonaparte, they would fall in love with him. At which the impressionable girls jumped into Home's cutter and asked to be rowed round the warship. They had to be put ashore.[25]

The same scenes were re-enacted after *Bellerophon* was moved to Plymouth. Among the visitors was Eastlake the painter who, according to Benjamin Haydon's diary, went out in a boat and 'made a small whole-length portrait'. The French officers gave him a certificate, declaring the painting to be *'très ressemblant, il a le mérite de donner une idée exacte de l'habitude du corps de [Napoleon I]'*. Although two guard ships had been ordered to take up station either side of Bonaparte's floating prison, and to keep off visitors by means of boat patrols, still those visitors came in greater and greater numbers, prompted by the hope of seeing this living legend and of being able to tell their children they had done so. The boats were so numerous that the naval patrols were incapable of keeping them off. 'I am certain I speak within bounds,' wrote Maitland, 'when I state that upward of a thousand were collected round the ship, in each of which, on average, there were not fewer than eight people. The crush was so great as to render it quite impossible for the guard boats to keep them off.' The sailors in *Bellerophon* took to displaying placards with information about where Bonaparte was and what he was doing: 'at breakfast', 'in the cabin with Captain Maitland', 'going to dinner', and, especially exciting for the spellbound crowds, 'coming on deck'. When eventually he did so, he responded in his habitual manner with salutes and taking off his hat.

Mrs Harriet Haviland, the sister of Benjamin Haydon, the painter and diarist, was among those who had themselves rowed out to *Bellerophon*, and wrote to her brother describing the scene and her own feelings:

> On Friday I went out to see Buonaparte, but the guard boats kept us at such great distance I was rather disappointed as it was impossible to clearly distinguish his features. He seems a good figure and dignified; and to the disgrace of Plymothians be it said, yesterday, as he withdrew, the people rose up in their boats and applauded him. There is so much that is mysterious and prepossessing about him now in his great

misfortunes, so much pity is felt that it is dangerous, I think, to the loyalty of the people to keep him here too long; they all seem fascinated. Napoleon has a large stomach, though not otherwise fat, he walks on deck between 5 and 6.[26]

Clearly, Mrs Haviland, an educated woman, disapproved of the crowd's enthusiasm, but what lay behind that enthusiasm, and what was in Napoleon's mind as he acknowledged the cheers? These are questions difficult to answer (see Introduction), but as regards the second point, a possible clue lies in what Lieutenant Bowerbank, one of *Bellerophon's* officers, recorded in his journal:

> upon his [Napoleon] quitting the gangway – many of the spectators cheered. Being close to him I immediately fixed my eyes on him and marked the workings of his countenance. I plainly perceived that he was mortified and displeased and not a little agitated, attributing the shout, and I believe justly, to the exultation which they felt at having him in our possession. After he had retired, we were told he was taken ill.[27]

If Bonaparte really was ill and apprehensive, he had good reason to be. Even the adoring Home, for whom the ex-Emperor could do no wrong, wondered what the impression of the circus-like atmosphere of the waterborne masses must have been on the central figure. 'From the enormous rush that was made from every part of the country,' he wrote, 'he must have conceived that he was as much admired by the English as by his beloved French.' However affable his behaviour in view of the crowds, he had reason to fear, even as he was doffing his hat, that his destiny was likely to be very different from earlier hopes of settling down as an English country squire – in any case a highly implausible prospect, given his temperament and previous career. Some days previously, while *Bellerophon* was still at Torbay, the London newspapers had been brought on board, and they did not make for comfortable reading for the French party.

The papers whose copies reached the ship were almost universally hostile, none more so than *The Times* and *The Courier*. The former, which throughout the Napoleonic period had consistently vilified him and supported the Bourbon cause, wrote of 'the ex-rebel . . . a man who has committed every species of crime in one country', of one whose 'propensity to mischief will continue as long as his life'. The leader-writer considered that Bonaparte should be delivered up 'to the justice of an injured Sovereign [Louis XVIII] and of a country which he has involved in every species of ruin'.[28] *The Courier* was more explicit and even more severe: 'We are responsible in the eyes of the world for his being kept in such safe custody that, though his life may be spared, he shall be as dead to all political purposes, to all the business and designs of this world as if he were no longer in existence.' The paper reported rumours that he would be sent to St Helena, there to be guarded by an English regiment designated expressly for the purpose.

Press comment on the captive's fate was largely along party lines. The Tory papers – supporters of Lord Liverpool's government – exulted in the 'ogre's' overthrow and prescribed harsh punishment, in some papers amounting to the death penalty, for someone who had cost the British nation so much in human and material sacrifice. The Whig press, in contrast, while refraining, for patriotic reasons, from espousing openly Bonapartist views, saw it as its duty to criticise the government whenever and wherever possible. When that criticism could be combined with a defence of human justice and the liberty of the individual, there was no justification for holding back. According to The *Morning Chronicle*, Bonaparte was entitled to *habeus corpus*: 'we object to no measure that is indispensable to public security, but let not the laws of England be violated.' The *St James's Chronicle*, also of Whiggish tendency, pleaded for magnanimity, on the grounds that 'Britain will be found incapable of trampling on a man who has no longer the power to resent it'.

The Times' editorial line received vehement support from an anonymous reader who signed himself 'Probus'. For this avenger, public execution was the only possible treatment for Bonaparte. But if that proved impracticable, then he should be sent to Haiti (the country of Toussaint l'Ouverture, black leader of a revolution against colonial France, who was captured, sent to France and died in prison in 1803, possibly by assassination). Probus was particularly outraged by the suggestion of St Helena as Bonaparte's place of exile. 'This man is to be suffered to escape *a second time* . . . now that we have paid for his guilt by a more lamentable waste of gallant lives than were ever before lost by us, in any single battle [i.e. Waterloo], now *we* are to become his protectors!' Another contributor to *The Times*, signing himself 'Vetus' (in fact one Edward Sterling), proclaimed the theory of 'No peace with Bonaparte', which meant, according to Sterling, enforcing the unconditional surrender of France and the restoration of the Bourbons. Such extreme views were warmly contested by Hazlitt, in the *Morning Chronicle*, who argued that they could only mean the stifling for ever of any hopes of peace. Hazlitt, while admitting Napoleon's faults of character, was an unrepentant Bonapartist.

The idea of invoking *habeus corpus* was taken up by an English constitutional lawyer called Capel Lofft, who claimed that Bonaparte in *Bellerophon* was within the protection of English law and therefore could only be deported after trial and sentence, a view vigorously rejected by *The Courier*, which contended that Bonaparte was a prisoner of war and as such was not entitled to *habeus corpus*. In addition to which he was a man who had broken his parole at Elba 'and involved Europe again in warfare and slaughter, for his own selfish and ambitious purposes'.

Events at Plymouth, off which *Bellerophon* now lay, suddenly took an unexpected turn. Anthony Mackenrot, a lawyer, formerly of the West Indies, arrived with a subpoena, issued by the

High Court, for Bonaparte to appear as witness in a libel case involving him, Mackenrot. The affair went back to 1807 in the West Indies when, according to Mackenrot, Sir Alexander Cochrane, Commander-in Chief of the North American station, had shown cowardice in not attacking a French squadron. Cochrane, who maintained that his ships were in no condition to fight, brought a libel case (eight years later), and now Mackenrot, as defendant, wanted Bonaparte to testify as to the condition of the French ships. This does not seem originally to have been, on Mackenrot's part, anything to do with Capel Lofft and the business of *habeus corpus* or with any other pro-Bonapartist attempt to have Bonaparte transferred to British soil, where a writ of *habeus corpus* could legitimately have been served. But Lofft learned of Mackenrot's initiative and encouraged him. The problem was how to serve the subpoena on Bonaparte.

Of this background the naval authorities knew nothing. Admiral Lord Keith had certainly had word that a writ of *habeus corpus* was on the way. Given the fact that Bonaparte was not on dry land, the obvious person on whom it would be served was himself, as Commander-in-Chief of the Channel Fleet, and hence the senior custodian of Bonaparte's person. To refuse service of the writ would be to defy the order of the Court. On being informed of the impending arrival of Mackenrot, he therefore had himself rowed out to HMS *Tonnant*, one of the ships guarding *Bellerophon*, which had, in an attempt to escape the crowd, been moved out to sea.

The tenacious Mackenrot hired a boat and pursued the admiral, causing the latter to quit *Tonnant* in favour of another of the warships. With Mackenrot still in pursuit, the seventy-year-old admiral clambered back into his barge and urged the crew to row as vigorously as possible. Finally, Keith managed to give Mackenrot the slip. Even that was not the end of this farce. The indefatigable Mackenrot, having failed with Keith, decided to serve his writ directly on Maitland. His little craft was prevented by a guard boat from approaching *Bellerophon*, and the disgruntled lawyer returned to Plymouth and addressed a letter to Keith, assuring the harassed officer that the matter was not going to be allowed to rest there.

In fact, where Mackenrot was concerned, it did rest there. But Capel Lofft and his supporters were not finished, despite the sustained attack on them by the Tory press. He wrote again to the *Morning Chronicle* on 3 August, stressing that to banish Bonaparte to St Helena would be a breach of Magna Carta and of the act of *habeus corpus*, as well as a violation of the Bill of Rights. *The Times* was having none of this, and brought up the case of Captain Wright. This naval officer had, some years before, been captured by the French, accused of promoting an anti-Napoleonic conspiracy and died in a French prison with his throat cut – suicide, said the French; murder, said the British. Bonaparte should be seen, said *The Times*, 'as the author of the dark and mysterious murder of Capt. Wright, his prisoner-of-war'. Probus also went back on the attack. In a letter to *The Times*, repeating his opposition to the St Helena idea, he recommended that if it had to be St Helena, 'this atrocious murderer should be loaded with irons and shut up for ever in a dungeon'.

Amid all this crossfire about the proper treatment of Bonaparte, Lord Liverpool's government was also beset with doubts and anxieties. Even before Napoleon's defeat at Waterloo, the allies, meeting at the Congress of Vienna, had declared him an outlaw, who 'as an enemy and disturber of the tranquillity of the world has rendered himself liable to public vengeance'. After Napoleon's abdication, but before he had given himself up to Maitland, Liverpool wrote to Castlereagh, the Foreign Secretary, expressing the wish that 'the King of France would hang or shoot Bonaparte as the best termination of the business'. But there was in the end no question of handing him over to the French. The Duke of Wellington's magnanimous instincts played their part here in ruling out any such course of action.*

Bonaparte could conceivably have been tried by the allies as an outlaw and war criminal, in what would have been an early nineteenth-century rehearsal of the Nuremberg trials. The difficulties about this and all other possibilities was that he had not been captured in battle but had voluntarily placed himself in Maitland's hands. Whatever the flowery and pretentious nature of the Themistocles letter (Croker, Secretary to the Admiralty, roared with laughter when he first heard of the reference to Themistocles), it did seem to establish the ex-Emperor's status as different from that of a straightforward prisoner of war, and certainly not as clear cut as the murderer-of-Captain-Wright school of thought would have it.

On 21 July, in a significant letter to Castlereagh, Liverpool summed up his government's views after it had received the news that Bonaparte was in British hands. 'We are all of the opinion,' he wrote, 'that it would not answer to confine him in this country.' He foresaw 'very nice legal questions' which would be 'particularly embarrassing'. Moreover, thought the Prime Minister, 'he would become an object of curiosity immediately' – this was before the arrival of *Bellerophon* at Torbay and the boatloads of sightseers – 'and possibly of compassion'.† So the best thing would be to send him to St

---

*He told Blücher, who wanted Napoleon shot, 'he and I had acted too distinguished parts in these transactions to become executioners . . . if the [allied and victorious] Sovereigns wished to put him to death, they should appoint an executioner which should not be me' (*Despatches of the Duke of Wellington*, ed. Colonel Gurwood, vol. XII, p. 516).

†An English historian, Felix Markham (in his foreword to M. Jean Duhamel's *The Fifty Days: Napoleon in England*, London, Hart-Davis, 1969), discerns in the behaviour of the crowds an element of tribute to a great man: 'Despite the never-ending wars to

27

Helena 'where the situation is particularly healthy'. At such a distance in such a place, Liverpool wrote, all intrigue would be impossible and 'being withdrawn so far from the European world, he would very soon be forgotten'.

The Prime Minister's prediction was wrong in two respects. In the longer term, it miscalculated or failed to foresee the growth of the Napoleonic legend: that assiduous rewriting of history, of myth-making, undertaken by Bonaparte and his staff at St Helena and later, which was to present to the world an idealised version of Napoleon's career and his (self-proclaimed) efforts to bring freedom and unity to Europe. As was to be expected, the legend took hold in France with far greater strength than it ever did in Britain, but even here it had its true believers and is still today cherished by some enthusiasts.

The second and more important respect in which Napoleon's cause won support lay in the attitude of the Whig aristocracy in 1815. Lord Holland and his formidable wife were foremost among those who sought to show that the government was treating Bonaparte unjustly. Hobhouse (later Lord Broughton) wrote that Napoleon's surrender 'had made ten times the sensation here than it has in Paris'. Sheridan, a long-standing Foxite and on-and-off friend of the Hollands, mocked the proceedings at Vienna, speaking of 'crowned scoundrels cutting up Europe like carcass-butchers and cruelly maltreating their subjects who had rescued them from Napoleon'. Hobhouse's final judgement on the dispatch of the defeated Emperor to St Helena can be taken as representative of the feelings of the small but

---

stop Napoleon's bid for world conquest, despite the crude war propaganda of the Tory Press, they sensed they were in the presence of a unique historical personality, and they were not unaware that Napoleon stood for the repudiation of oligarchy and the career open to talents.' As there can be no way of knowing what exactly the crowds were thinking of, it seems more likely that it is Markham who was not unaware of these things.

distinguished number of English Bonapartists in 1815: 'so ends the greatest man in modern times, overwhelmed by a monstrous coalition . . .'[29]

Hobhouse was a passionate admirer of Napoleon. Against all advice, he managed to get to Paris in April 1815 (after Napoleon's return from Elba), and on being asked by the Town Major of Valenciennes why he was going to Paris, just as most Englishmen were leaving France as fast as they could, he replied, 'solely to see your Emperor'. He succeeded in his purpose, standing close to Napoleon at a military review in the Tuileries, when he found his eyes watering 'at the sight of the world's wonder'. 'I am not astonished or ashamed,' he wrote, 'at having experienced such feelings at the sight of the man who has played the most extraordinary, gigantic part of any human being in ancient and modern times.' There is no reason to question the sincerity and steadfastness of Hobhouse's views.

One extreme Whig and Napoleonist had already yielded to the temptation of suicide. Samuel Whitbread, heir to a vast brewing fortune and the champion not only of Napoleon but of Princess Caroline, the estranged wife of the Prince Regent, considered that Napoleon was an unstoppable force whom it would be better to treat with than to oppose. In the Commons on 3 April 1815 he had sharply criticised the government for the fact that Wellington at Vienna had signed the declaration branding Napoleon as an enemy and disturber of world peace. Whitbread's motion was rejected, but after Waterloo, displaying the inconsistency that characterised so many British Bonapartists, he voted in favour of a huge monetary grant to the victorious Wellington. Then, the day after Paris capitulated to the allies, he committed suicide by cutting his throat. He had been showing increasing signs of mental instability, but even allowing for this and for his financial difficulties there is little doubt that Napoleon's defeat was a major reason for his act of desperation. Bonaparte, who was remarkably alive to the strength (or weakness) of his potential supporters in Parliament, knew about Whitbread's violent end and questioned W.H. Lyttelton, a Whig MP, about it when the two met aboard HMS *Northumberland*, the ship that was to transport Napoleon to St Helena.

Meanwhile, with Bonaparte still an unwilling prisoner in *Bellerophon*, the government in London sought to define his status as a preliminary to deciding finally what to do with him. The Lord Chancellor, Lord Eldon, was appealed to. Working in conjunction with the Lord Chief Justice, the Master of the Rolls and the principal law officers of the Crown, he prepared a memorandum, according to which Bonaparte could be considered a prisoner of war. Soon afterwards, arrangements were set in train to convey him to St Helena.‡ The decision was transmitted to him verbally by Keith and Major-General Sir Henry Bunbury, Under-Secretary for War, on 31 July. The meeting was dominated by Napoleon's fervent protests, in which he accused Maitland of having entrapped him, said he refused to go to St Helena, prophesised that if he did go he would be dead in three months, and that the government would have disgraced itself in the eyes of Europe. All his visitors could do was to listen and undertake to convey the substance of his outburst to their political masters.

The meeting could not fail to have been a painful one for Keith and Bunbury. The former, as we have seen, had been fascinated by his first meeting with Bonaparte. Besides, he felt a sense of personal obligation. His nephew, James Drummond

‡St Helena is an island in the South Atlantic, 700 miles south-east of Ascension (the nearest land), 1,695 miles north-west of Cape Town and 4,477 miles from Southampton. Although it lies within the tropics, the climate is temperate. St Helena was a possession of the British East India Company from the middle of the seventeenth century onwards. In 1834 it became the property of the Crown.

Elphinstone, a captain in the 7th Hussars, had been seriously wounded and taken prisoner in the fighting that immediately preceded Waterloo. Napoleon, made aware of this capture, had given orders for the prisoner to receive medical attention, which probably saved his life. In a letter to Maitland, delivered soon after *Bellerophon's* arrival at Torbay, Keith had conveyed his 'greatest possible obligations to him [Napoleon] for his attentions to my nephew'. Bunbury did not have this personal link, but he did, unlike Keith, have decent French and thus it fell to him to translate the letter containing the government's decision. Bunbury must have done his job adequately, because Bonaparte, when asked by Keith if he wanted a written translation of the letter, said he had understood it perfectly. In answer to Bonaparte's protestations, Bunbury gave the stock official response – in this it was true – that he was only the messenger and was not authorised to enter into discussions. The cautious Bunbury was even unwilling to confirm Keith's semi-assurance to the captive that once *Northumberland* had appeared, there could be a delay before Bonaparte was required to embark in her. In a note that Bunbury made about Bonaparte's personal demeanour, he recorded that 'his expression was serious and almost melancholy, and showed no sign of anger or strong emotion'.

Two days after this awkward encounter the representatives of the allied powers (Britain, Austria, Russia and Prussia) signed an agreement in Paris about Bonaparte's future. According to this, 'his custody is especially entrusted to the British Government. The choice of the place, and of the measures which can best secure the object of the present stipulation, is reserved to His Britannic Majesty'. Whatever difficulties might still persist over the interpretation of English law and practice – difficulties that Capel Lofft and his friends had already fastened on to – the Paris agreement provided international approval for any treatment that London might choose to mete out to Bonaparte.

That at least seems a justifiable conclusion to be drawn today. The Whig§ newspapers of the time did not take this view at all. The *Morning Chronicle* laid it down that 'no man, however criminal, can be transported without a judgement'. Bonaparte, the paper's writer thought, 'being within the jurisdiction of the Admiralty, is entitled to *Habeus Corpus*'. In the same issue, the ever-active Capel Lofft had a letter maintaining that though not on British soil, Napoleon's presence at Plymouth meant that 'he is in a British country . . . *Habeus Corpus*, if issued, must be obeyed'. The *Chronicle* announced that it had received over a hundred letters from all over England, and claimed that Lofft's letters had 'evidently made a strong sensation'. It predicted – accurately, as it turned out – that the government would seek an Act of Parliament to indemnify it against what the newspaper considered an illegal act. An answer was swift in coming to these arguments. In that evening's issue of *The Courier*, which referred to Bonaparte as 'the tyrant of the human race', the writer unleashed all his venom: Bonaparte was 'the violator of all laws', a 'ferocious and dangerous animal' and, more prosaically, a prisoner of war. Later in August, as *Northumberland* set sail for St Helena, the paper bade him farewell in no less vituperative terms. To those who regretted Bonaparte's humiliation and fall, the writer addressed a reminder that they were pitying 'a tyrant who had threatened to make this great and glorious land a territory unfit for the residence of human beings',

§I have taken the term 'Whig' to mean those people, and publications, who upheld the principles of the Glorious Revolution of 1688, and thus tended to be opponents of despotic royal regimes in Europe. The term 'Tory' (not in general use until later than the Whig label) came to apply to those who supported the King's government and all constituted authority. It would, however, be misleading to suggest that all Tories were for harshness towards Bonaparte and all Whigs sympathetic to his plight.

a tyrant 'who has been the cause of the death of hundreds of thousands of human beings', etc., etc. Even though *The Courier* admitted that 'Napoleon was one of the most extraordinary characters' – it was extraordinary how often the word 'extra-ordinary' was used by friend and foe alike to describe him – it had no doubt that he was getting the fate he deserved.

An anonymous reviewer in the (Tory-sympathising) *Quarterly Review*, writing about a number of books recently published on St Helena and the Emperor's downfall, was in no doubt about what ought to be done to him. His custody is 'a very ticklish point', because whatever Britain does, she will be blamed; 'if he be not actually confined, he may, and probably will, escape; if he be confined, we shall have all the oppositions in Europe crying shame'. The writer argues that, instead of the allied governments' 'weak, indiscreet, unjust and unjustifiable' policies – i.e. entrusting Bonaparte's custody to Britain, which then sent him to St Helena – he should have been executed. This would have been the 'forfeit of his rebellion against the King of France and his treason against all the nations of Europe'. But as things are, the reviewer concludes, it is import-ant not to make the prisoner too comfortable – 'a great deal too much attention has already been shown him'.

The decision to order *Bellerophon* to sea, there to await *Northumberland's* arrival (she was taking on stores at Portsmouth), was prompted by several fears. Among them was the danger that somehow or other the Capel Lofft lobby would succeed in serving a writ of *habeus corpus*, or that Bonaparte might try to escape and might succeed. Maitland had a scare on 3 August, when it was rumoured that the previous night a boat had been seen under *Bellerophon's* stern. Bonaparte had not been at breakfast the following morning, and when a midshipman was ordered to go out on the boom and look through the windows of his day cabin, he reported that there was no one to be seen. Maitland enquired of the suite about Bonaparte's whereabouts and Bertrand said that he was ill and keeping to his cabin. This proved to be the truth, but it still left Maitland and Keith in a jumpy frame of mind.

The latter wrote in his diary that he was 'worried to death with idle folk coming, even from Glasgow, to see him [Bonaparte] . . . there is no nation so foolish as we are'. His anxiety seemed to have banished whatever sympathy he may earlier have felt for his prisoner, for his journal also contains a reference to the bad behaviour of the crowds, which 'obliged me to put to sea with this Reptile to await the arrival of Sir George Cockburn' (the admiral flying his flag in *Northumberland*). The transfer of the French party would then take place at sea, away from the curious gaze of the crowds or the importunities of meddlesome lawyers. *Northumberland* duly arrived, and on 10 August Bonaparte, together with those of his companions whom he had chosen to go with him to St Helena, left *Bellerophon*, where they had spent nearly a month of uncertainty and anguish, and boarded *Northumberland*. He took his time doing so, to the extent that Cockburn, who had gone with Keith to escort Bonaparte to *Northumberland*, grew impatient. Keith reprimanded his fellow admiral: 'much greater men than either you or I have waited longer for him before now – let him take his time.'

But before the transfer took place, there were further objections and accusations from the French. First came Napoleon himself, with 'a solemn protest, in the face of heaven and of men', against the St Helena decision. It was cast in the high-flown style of the Themistocles letter and was clearly designed as much for perusal by posterity as for contemporary reading. Indeed, the choice of words virtually admits as much: 'I appeal to history – it will say that an enemy, who for twenty years waged war against the English people, came voluntarily, in his misfortunes, to seek an asylum under their laws . . . what return did England make for so much magnanimity? They feigned to stretch forth a friendly hand to that enemy, and when he had delivered himself up in good faith, they sacrificed him.'

'Feigned to stretch forth a friendly hand' is a phrase with a certain resonance, but its content is irreconcilable with what took place off Rochefort in mid-July. Maitland, it is true, had suggested asylum in England, but he also made it plain that the ex-Emperor 'must consider himself at the disposal of His Royal Highness the Prince Regent'. It is impossible to resist the conclusion that the 'appeal to history' protest was exactly that; as Las Cases later wrote, it was 'to be a weapon in the hands of our friends, and leave causes of remembrance as well as grounds of defence with the public'.

In the highly charged atmosphere created by the circumstances, it was hardly surprising that some bitter words, in addition to formal protestations, should be exchanged. Maitland was none the less taken aback when Las Cases, walking the deck of *Bellerophon* with him, alleged that during their conversations off Rochefort, he, Maitland, had given assurances that Bonaparte would be well received in England and would be allowed to stay there. Maitland instantly repudiated any such allegation and later, in his account of his dealings with Bonaparte's emissaries, accused Las Cases of duplicity, in that, on first boarding *Bellerophon*, he had pretended not to speak English. Maitland thought this was for the purpose 'of throwing me off my guard, that he might take advantage of any expressions that fell from me'. He continued to assert, then and subsequently, that he had said no more than he had no reason to suppose that 'he [Bonaparte] would not be well received'. According to Maitland's report to Keith, when he complained to Montholon about Las Cases' accusations, Montholon said that Las Cases was a disappointed man who 'attributes the Emperor's situation to himself'.

Montholon also told Maitland that Napoleon 'feels convinced that you have acted like a man of honour throughout'. That this was not just flattery is proved by Bonaparte's wish to give him a portrait of himself, set in diamonds, which Maitland was obliged to refuse. Montholon understood his reasons for refusal, but conveyed the ex-Emperor's 'thanks for the manner in which you have conducted yourself throughout this whole affair'. Bonaparte himself repeated something similar as he left *Bellerophon* to transfer to *Northumberland*, by asking Maitland to tell *Bellerophon's* officers of his gratitude for the way in which he had been treated. To Maitland personally, in the last private meeting between the two men before the transfer to *Northumberland*, Bonaparte spoke in yet more generous terms. 'My reception in England,' he said, 'has been very different from what I expected, but it gives me much satisfaction to assure you that I feel your conduct to me throughout has been that of a gentleman and a man of honour.'[30]

Despite all the previous arguments, claims and counterclaims, accusations and repudiations, the fact remains that courtesy prevailed at the end, to the great credit of all concerned. In the final encounter between Keith and Bonaparte, the latter once more declared that he refused to leave *Bellerophon*: 'you must take me by force.' With tact and dignity, Keith replied that he hoped 'you will not reduce an officer like me to do so disagreeable an act as to use force against your person.' 'No,' Bonaparte assured him, but 'you shall order me.' Which Keith proceeded to do, adding that his barge was waiting and Bonaparte was not to hurry. Finally, the prisoner and his party boarded the barge, which set off for *Northumberland*.

Maitland, watching it recede, as the *Bellerophon's* ship's company was also doing, said to his servant, 'what do people say of him?' The man replied that he had that very morning overheard some of the sailors discussing their passenger, and one of them had said 'they may abuse that man as much as they please, but if the people of England knew him as well as we do, they would not hurt a hair of his head', to which the others had agreed. The mutual respect between Napoleon and the Royal Navy, which had its beginnings in *Bellerophon*, and was continued during the long voyage to St Helena, thus becomes an established fact, to the honour of both parties.

Maitland closes this unprecedented chapter of dramatic events in words that admirably sum up the reactions towards Napoleon of that very small portion of the British people which had had personal experiences of and contact with the defeated superman; reactions founded partly on the image of a fallen idol but also on natural, humane feelings. He wrote:

> It may appear surprising that the possibility could exist of a British officer being prejudiced in favour of one who had caused so many calamities to his country; but to such an extent did he possess the power of pleasing, that there are few people who could have sat at the same table with him for nearly a month, as I did, without feeling a sensation of pity, allied perhaps to regret, that a man possessed of so many fascinating qualities, and who had held so high a situation in life, should be reduced to the situation in which I saw him.[31]

Noble words, especially from someone who for week after week in that summer of 1815 had been subjected to the pressures and anxieties that Captain Maitland, RN, had had to undergo.

Maitland, of course, had had prolonged personal experience of Bonaparte's company and character. The vast majority of British people had not – even those thousands of curious sightseers who had themselves rowed out to *Bellerophon*. For the historian, trying to describe the feelings at a given time of a large number of people, let alone a whole nation, is a daunting and often impossible task. H.A.L. Fisher, himself an authority on Napoleon and his age, did not flinch from it. He considered the Corsican 'the greatest soldier and administrator in history',[32] but as regards popular opinion,

> Englishmen viewed Napoleon, not with complete justification but also not without justification, as the tyrant who respected no pledge, stopped short of no ambition, and flinched before no crime. They thought of him not as the creator of nationalities (for he created none in his lifetime) but as the destroyer of principles and the enemy of constitutional freedom all over

the world. As the men of the first century regarded Attila the Hun, so, with a few exceptions, did the contemporaries of Pitt and Liverpool regard Napoleon.[33]

2

A Helping Hand from
Holland House

As *Northumberland* conveyed Bonaparte and his companions to their exile in St Helena – a voyage lasting sixty-
seven days, during which, as in *Bellerophon*, he established a
warm relationship with most of the officers and men – his
friends and admirers in England set to work, as best they might,
on his behalf. Foremost among them were Henry Richard Fox,
third Baron Holland and nephew of Charles James Fox, and his
wife, Elizabeth, née Vassall. She had previously been married to
and divorced from Sir Godfrey Webster, whom she had married
when she was fifteen and he forty-nine.

We have already encountered the Hollands in Paris in 1802,
when both Lord Holland and his uncle were received by the
First Consul. Their ambivalent impressions on that occasion
were typical of the doubts that assailed these pillars of Whig – it
would be more accurate to say Foxite – society whenever they
came up against the conundrum of Bonapartism. Was it a force
for good or evil? Was Napoleon the heir to the French Revolution
and could that Revolution, in overthrowing monarchical despotism, be compared with the triumph of the Glorious Revolution
of 1688 in England?

This argument, in various forms, continues to this day.* After the achievements and disorder of the French Revolution, Napoleon's emergence as a soldier, administrator, law-giver, stabiliser, his dazzling gifts as an inspirer of men and ideas, his partial success at creating a new and unified Europe (albeit under French domination): all these elements combine to make him, for many, an object of wonder and respect, tending towards veneration. On the other hand, his record as a spiller of blood on a vast scale, as one who held the value of human life in perpetual contempt, whose personal ambitions grew in proportion to his conquests, whose disingenuous attempts, at the end of his life, to justify his career as the triumph of light over darkness, make him one of the most notable self-apologists of history: this list should be enough to repel – it certainly repels me – even the most ardent admirer of strong leadership and mastery of events. It is hardly surprising if the Foxite Whigs had their doubts from time to time. Nor is it always easy to distinguish their genuine enthusiasm for the fallen Emperor from their wish to embarrass and discredit their political opponents in Government.†

A distinction must be made here between, on the one hand, Lord Holland and what was generally called the Holland House set, and on the other, Lady Holland. The latter's admiration for Napoleon knew no bounds. Reservations or misgivings, which

*At the time, it found its most dramatic expression in the disagreement between Fox and Edmund Burke, the latter as fearful of the consequences of the French Revolution as the former, at least initially, was enthusiastic.

†Someone who never wavered in his admiration of Napoleon and in his disgust at the way he was treated was George Home, the young midshipman serving in *Bellerophon*. Writing twenty-two years after the events of 1815 (*Memoirs of an Aristocrat*, p. 254) he was still boiling with rage over what, he prophesied, 'will be a vile stain upon our name to the latest ages'.

often beset her husband, were foreign to the mind of this intemperate, imperious romantic. After 1815 there stood, in the gardens of Holland House, a bust of the Emperor by Canova, around whose base ran the following quatrain:

> He is not dead, he breathes the air
> in distant lands beyond the deep,
> Some distant sea-girt island where
> harsh men the hero keep.

Other busts of the 'hero' adorned the rooms of the house, including one beneath which Lady Holland had placed the specimens of iron ore sent to her by Napoleon from Elba, in response to her bundle of English newspapers. No religious shrine or icon could have conveyed a more profound message of reverent admiration.

Elizabeth Vassall/Holland was from youth onwards a controversial figure. By all accounts one of the most beautiful women of her time, she was free with her affections; in the period preceding her divorce, during which she spent five nearly unbroken years (1791–6) in France, Switzerland and Italy, she had affairs with at least four young Englishmen doing the Grand Tour.[1] Macaulay described her in 1831, in words that would have been almost as appropriate fifteen years earlier: 'she is a bold-looking woman, with the remains of a fine figure, and the air of Queen Elizabeth. A great lady, fanciful, hysterical and hypochondrial, ill-natured and good-natured, sceptical and superstitious, afraid of ghosts and not of god, would not for the world begin a journey on a Friday and thought nothing of running away from her husband.'[2] The husband in question was Webster. She never had any inclination to leave Holland. Despite their different natures and prejudices, they shared much in common, including, and above all, a love of Continental travel and languages. To Holland House and its reputation as a centre of Foxite gatherings, gossip and Bonapartism, she brought not only enthusiasm but an unshakable resolve to have her own way.

41

Supreme in her own mansion and family, she exercised a singular and seemingly capricious tyranny, even over guests of the highest rank – capricious it seemed but there was in reality *intention* in all she did; and this intention was the maintenance of power which she gained and strenuously used, though not without discretion in fixing its limits.[3]

She must have been impressive and intimidating. Sydney Smith, an habitué of Foxite occasions, joked that chemists in London took to making up pills especially for people who had been frightened at Holland House.

Lord Holland's attitude towards Napoleon and Bonapartism in general was, in contrast to his wife's, a good deal more discriminating: 'From the moment that their [Charles James Fox's and Holland's] interview with Bonaparte in 1802 was interrupted by a delegation from the Senate asking him to become Consul for life, the opinions of Holland and his uncle became a compound of admiration and deep suspicion.'[4]

The French Revolution was indisputably anti-monarchical, and that in itself was enough to kindle the spark of approval in Foxite breasts. The executions of the French King and Queen were regrettable, but so, in Holland's view, was the partition of Poland, the work of kingly regimes in St Petersburg, Vienna and Berlin. Robespierre and the Terror found no favour at Holland House, but nor did Britain's entry into the war against France in 1793, as the allies of the autocratic systems of these three kingdoms. Napoleon's advent to power, despite its dictatorial aspects, meant a new and welcome stability for France and a sweeping away of earlier, despotic rule. But as Lady Holland's hero advanced from Consul to Emperor, as a new form of autocratic power emerged in all its true colours, so Holland retreated into ambivalence. He told his sister Caroline in 1814 that 'I hate and detest Bonaparte more than ever and yet I am not sure that if he were to fall the legitimate sovereign would not be restored [i.e. the Bourbons] and that in my mind is the last of misfortunes – bad for France, for liberty and for mankind'.[5] As between Napoleon and the Bourbons, there could be only one choice.

Waterloo and the dispatch of Bonaparte to St Helena did little or nothing to change these feelings. Already, Napoleon's reverses and retreats from 1812 onwards had disconcerted the Hollands. His confrontation with what Holland called 'the northern barbarians' – Russia and Prussia – had left the Foxites with no alternative but to sympathise with him. During the months leading up to the first abdication (1814), the Hollands were once again indulging their favourite pastime of Continental travel. In southern Italy they were due to visit the Greek temples at Paestum, but Holland told his sister that 'the escape of the hero has set Lady Holland's spirits in such a flurry and agitation that I suspect she will not be calm and sedate enough to enjoy the imposing gravity of Dorick architecture'.[6] Writing again to the same sister after Waterloo, he explains that though he welcomes peace, 'if it comes with the triumph of kings and the restoration of the Bourbons it comes as much embittered to my palate as so sweet a thing can be'.

Holland's almost visceral antipathy to kings led him, late in life, to publish his *Foreign Reminiscences*,[7] a book generally condemned by reason of its biased treatment of monarchs, for its lack of balance; even the Whig *Edinburgh Review* had to admit that such criticisms were mostly well founded. But it is interesting in revealing Holland's sentiments, even though he is writing decades after Napoleon's death, about his abdication and exile to St Helena. Holland absolves Maitland of any artifice over the manner of Napoleon's surrender but goes on to describe the St Helena decision as 'ungenerous' and Napoleon as 'this great prisoner'. He also recorded his opinion that the mere existence, in however imprecise a form, of the idea of St Helena as a place of exile was enough, when Napoleon became aware of it while still at Elba (from the newspapers supplied to him there by Lady Holland), to absolve him of all previous international obligations and to justify him in trying to recover his lost empire.

Whether these thoughts made Holland 'an incorrigible Jacobin', as his fellow Whig Thomas Grenville called him, he certainly regretted the consequences of Waterloo. Aided and abetted by his wife,[‡] he embarked on a campaign to mitigate the conditions of Bonaparte's detention. The first and principal weapon was the dinner table at Holland House, that gathering place regarded by its critics and enemies as the abode of cranks and traitors, but by its admirers as the fount of wisdom and true liberal spirit. In late August 1815 a dinner-party was assembled which included Samuel Rogers and Henry Luttrell, both members of the inner circle, Lord Ossulston, a Whig grandee who incidentally had helped to revise the rules of cricket, the Hon. Frederick North, a former Governor of Ceylon, and, most important, Sir Hudson Lowe. He had recently been appointed Governor of St Helena, which meant in effect that he was to be Bonaparte's custodian (French historians generally use the word gaoler).

This officer, who, for his real or alleged treatment of Napoleon, has been reviled alike by most French historians and British Bonapartists, was in 1815 a relatively unknown personality, although he had been until recently quartermaster-general to the Duke of Wellington's armies in the Low Countries. The Hollands' strategy was to win him over to their side before he assumed his duties at St Helena. He was to prove a harder nut to crack than Colonel Neil Campbell, the British Commissioner at Elba during Napoleon's time there, whom Lady Holland had

[‡]Harriet, Countess Granville, was twice at Holland House in the late summer of 1815. After the first visit (21 July), she wrote to her sister that 'she [Lady Holland] was seated on the grass . . . very cross and absurd about Bonaparte, "poor dear man" as she calls him'. She was there again in September, when she described the Hollands' politics as 'reduced to adoration of Bonaparte'. (*Letters of Harriet, Countess Granville, 1810–1845,* ed. F. Leveson Gower, 2 vols, London, Longmans, 1894).

courted successfully to the point that Campbell had allowed her to send the bundle of English newspapers to the Emperor. Lowe was entertained at Holland House no fewer than eight times in the autumn of 1815. Among his fellow guests on these occasions were the Prince Regent's brother, the Duke of York, and various real or potential Bonapartist sympathisers, including Byron and his wife, both of them mutually disenchanted after only eight months of marriage. Byron asked Lowe whether Napoleon had the qualities of a great general. Lowe, whose military career had been less than meteoric, replied that his qualities were 'very simple'. 'I had always thought,' wrote Byron later, 'that a degree of simplicity was an element of greatness.'

The Hollands were not making much headway with Lowe. The latter, during the course of his Holland House dinners, had received the government's directive for Bonaparte's treatment at St Helena. The instructions were detailed and consisted for the most part of far-reaching arrangements to prevent Napoleon from escaping or making unauthorised contact with the outer world. Thus, all letters addressed to him or to his entourage would have first to be delivered to and read by the Admiral or the Governor, and all letters to 'the General' from abroad must first be sent to the Secretary of State for War and the Colonies (Lord Bathurst). Bonaparte must always, in his movements, be accompanied by an officer appointed by the Admiral or the Governor. Bonapartists of all kinds[§] have tended to argue that these precautions were excessive and oppressive. But what else

[§]Notably M. Gilbert Martineau, for many years French Consul at St Helena, a Napoleonist of the first order, and keeper of the shrine at Longwood. In *Napoleon surrenders* (English translation John Murray, London, 1971, p. 188), he makes the curious suggestion that if these instructions had been 'addressed to a man of good family' they would have been 'theoretically valuable'. This appears to be another version of the complaint that Lowe was no gentleman.

could a government be expected to do when internationally charged with the custody of the biggest threat to peace in Europe, who had already shown his capacity to plot and execute an escape? In any case, the instructions need to be read in conjunction with the covering letter, which states the Prince Regent's desires 'that no greater measure of security with respect to confinement or restriction be imposed than what is deemed necessary for . . . the perfect security of General Bonaparte's person'.#

Soon after his eighth dinner at Holland House, Lowe, who had meanwhile married a colonel's widow, departed for St Helena. Lady Holland had failed to obtain from him any concessions enabling her to send books, newspapers and other little comforts direct to Bonaparte at St Helena. (A little later, according to *Foreign Reminiscences*, she tried to arrange, knowing that Bonaparte liked to drink water and wine extremely cold, for 'a newly invented machine for making ice' to be dispatched to St Helena. She even told Lord Bathurst where to buy it, but nothing happened.) Nor did the Hollands' efforts to aid and protect other former French supporters of the ex-Emperor meet with much success. The ultra-royalists were in the ascendant in France, bent on revenge. Although those who had borne arms for Napoleon were supposed to be guaranteed immunity, it was ruled that this provision did not apply to the court-martial trying Marshal Ney. He was condemned to death. His wife, La Maréchale, addressed an appeal to the Prince Regent, sending a copy to Holland. Holland approached the

---

#In the voluminous correspondence that from 1816 to 1821 passed between Lowe in St Helena and Bathurst in London, constant emphasis is laid on the need to ensure that Bonaparte is provided with 'every relaxation and indulgence in any way conducive to his health and comfort, so long as they are not incompatible with the security of his person'. (Bathurst's letter of 21 February 1817 in ADD MSS 20119).

Prime Minister, Lord Liverpool, who advised him to go direct to the Regent. The latter was out of London, and before long La Maréchale had her answer from Wellington: it was a matter for the French government. Ney was executed by firing squad, refusing a blindfold.

By this time Bonaparte had arrived at St Helena, and his sympathisers in England redoubled their efforts to prove that he was being held illegally. Capel Lofft, undeterred by his lack of success over *habeus corpus*, addressed a series of letters to Holland, urging the latter to argue Bonaparte's case in Parliament and inviting him to recruit to the cause various Whig grandees, including another of the Prince Regent's brothers, the Duke of Sussex. To detain Bonaparte, Lofft argued, was in breach of 'the known laws of nations'; so great a power (of imprisonment) 'is sufficient for any individual over any other . . . it makes the habitable globe a Bastille, to one cell or other of which this wonderful individual [Bonaparte] is to be transferred at the pleasure of an officer of the government'.

Information now began to accrue, and to be published in the public prints, about Bonaparte's arrival and behaviour at St Helena. From October 1815 onwards, the London papers, notably the *Morning Chronicle* (Whig and Bonapartist) and *The Times* (Tory and anti-Bonapartist) began publishing extracts from letters and reports reaching them from the island. Who the messengers were who conveyed these missives is not always clear, but as subsequent developments showed, there was never any lack of couriers – ships' captains, passengers on transit ships calling at St Helena on the voyage from the Far East, and others. The *Morning Chronicle* on 15 October ran an article headed 'Authentic particulars of Bonaparte, from an officer on board *Northumberland*'. This consisted of a long account of Bonaparte's conduct and conversation during the voyage, bearing out the contention that all went smoothly and that Cockburn (the Admiral) and Bonaparte were 'on excellent terms'.[8]

A further piece from St Helena, this time from the surgeon of *Northumberland*, is given in the *Morning Chronicle* on 28 December, in which the writer speaks of the utter dreariness of the island and of how the captive is writing a protest to London. Earlier, at the beginning of December, the editorialist of the same paper weighed in with some stinging comments about how the government had now lost the scapegoat on whom they had found it convenient to lay all blame. *The Times,* for its part, compiled an article (12 February 1816) based on 'accounts received from St Helena', according to which 'the late Usurper of the French throne' was surrounded by restrictions and precautions to prevent, 'the possibility of a second attempt of this restless being to create insurrection and disturb the repose of the continent'. A month previously *The Times* had published an extract 'from a gentleman just returned from India' whose ship had called at St Helena. From this, it is clear that the same degree of curiosity about Bonaparte prevailed at St Helena as it had at Plymouth and Torbay. The traveller describes how he and his companion rode up to Longwood one afternoon and 'had the good fortune to arrive as [Bonaparte] was taking his afternoon's walk in his garden'. They tied up their horses and hid behind a bush. The ex-Emperor 'passed within a few feet of us' and they found that 'there was nothing in his appearance at all indicative of the great qualities he possesses'.

As St Helena was the stopping place for nearly all vessels making the journey from India and the Far East to England, so a visit to Longwood, in the hope of seeing or with luck talking to the illustrious captive, became for the transients almost an obligation, comparable to viewing the Taj Mahal or the pyramids. Gourgaud, in his journal,[9] speaks of many English ladies and gentlemen disembarking from India.

> They arrive [at Longwood] at four o'clock to the number of 15 or 20, among whom are a Judge, Mr Burrows, Mr Arbuthnot and his wife . . . I complain to the Judge about the narrowness of the limits [within which Bonaparte is permitted

to go unescorted]. He replies that His Majesty is still too much to be feared, and that if one granted him the whole of the island for a residence, he wouldn't be long in escaping. The Emperor goes into the garden, where he receives the English people. They are delighted. His Majesty speaks to the Judge, who cries 'Ah, he is indeed a sovereign' . . . [next day] More Englishmen are presented to His Majesty. They are amazed. They came expecting to see a tiger, and they find a man.

The accounts of life at St Helena, which enliven the London papers throughout the years of Bonaparte's detention, are proof enough that English feelings – one learns less about what people in Scotland were thinking – were still divided about his fate. On the theory of out of sight, out of mind, it might be assumed that now that peace had been restored and the ex-Emperor banished, the majority of people put the past behind them and ceased to think much, or at all, about the man from Corsica. This is probably true, but in that case the strength of his English admirers' feelings, even if they represented only a small minority, is attested by the high Tory Sir Walter Scott's disgust at the way in which Napoleon, in 1815, was already becoming a hero to some people: 'to hear the nonsense which people talk in London about the alteration of that man's nature and disposition is enough to make a dog sick.'[10] Scott, though less abrasive when he came to write his multi-volume *Life of Napoleon*, is mocking about his humble origins: 'from a low isle/his lowlier lineage came'. ('Don Roderick', canto xxxix, about the usurpation of the Spanish Crown by Napoleon).*

*In fact, the Bonaparte family had, for whatever it was worth, an ancient title of nobility granted by the Genoese Republic, to which Corsica belonged up to 1768. Noble by birth Napoleon may have been, but a more realistic version of the family's circumstances is given in Evangeline Bruce's *Napoleon and Josephine* (Weidenfeld and Nicolson, 1995), where she describes the young Napoleon, on a visit to Corsica in 1786, finding his younger siblings, 'four future Kings, Queens and imperial highnesses running barefoot with the family herd of goats'.

Parliament reassembled in February 1816, just when these first reports from St Helena were coming to hand. Holland, conscious that he could not expect much support from his fellow Whigs, limited himself at this stage to attacking the post-Napoleonic peace treaties, which restored the Bourbons to the French throne. In a fine stream of Foxite opprobrium, he described them as 'a general and perpetual guarantee of all European governments against the governed'. In the preceding debate, the Prime Minister, Lord Liverpool, anticipating that the provisions of the treaties could be said to authorise interference in France's internal affairs, argued that there would be no stability in Europe unless there was such interference, its purpose being 'to put down the principle of universal empire and military despotism, which the power of France was so long employed to promote'. To this anti-Bonapartist thrust, Holland replied that sending Bonaparte to St Helena was unjustifiable and ungenerous and that he would not have received such treatment 'had he been descended from a line of Princes'.

Holland could have cited, had he so wished, an earlier example of British treatment of a captured French leader. On the field of Agincourt (1415), Charles Duc d'Orléans, nephew of Charles VI, King of France, and father of Louis XII, was taken prisoner and conveyed to England. Though treated there with the respect due to a great French Prince, for twenty-five years he was never anything but a prisoner, unable to plan or control his own movements as he was transferred from castle to castle. Nevertheless, he managed to hawk and hunt and above all to write some very fine poetry. This was hardly the régime Napoleon imagined for himself in England, though no doubt it would have been preferable to St Helena.

On 8 April Holland moved on to the main attack, with a dissenting opinion in the Lords on the bill, then before Parliament, 'for the more effective detaining in custody of Bonaparte'. He had previously asked for the Law Lords to be present to define the legal position. Could Bonaparte legally and realistically be considered a prisoner of war? Lord Lauderdale (Captain Maitland's relative) reiterated this question and added, with a striking lack of realism, that it would have been possible to keep Bonaparte securely in England 'in the custody of a police officer'. But the Lord Chancellor, Eldon, swept these arguments aside, insisting that the bill was 'plain and distinct', and it was passed accordingly. Holland entered his protest:

> because without reference to the character of previous conduct of the person who is the object of the present Bill, I disapprove of the measure which it sanctions and continues . . . to confine to distant exile and imprisonment a foreign and captive chief who, after the abdication of this authority, relying on British generosity, has surrendered himself to us in preference to his other enemies, is unworthy of a great country; and the Treaties by which after his captivity we bound ourselves to detain him in custody at the will of the Sovereigns to whom he had never surrendered himself, appear to me repugnant to the rules of equity and utterly uncalled for by expedience or necessity.

The Duke of Sussex, a friend and frequenter of Holland House, wished to be associated with the protest and was considerably put out when he found that Holland had gone ahead without consulting him. It was not too late, however, for his wish to be gratified, and his signature – Augustus Frederick – was added to the protest. If Holland, by reason of his radical views and his still more radical and overpowering wife, could be considered something of an oddity, Sussex, a royal prince, was even more eccentric.

The sixth son of George III, he was enormously tall and burly, suffered from asthma, always wore a black skullcap, was well read and an ardent supporter of political reform and Catholic emancipation, and was always boasting (and producing vocal evidence) of what he called his three-octave voice. His Whiggish principles and practices, which lay behind his support of Holland's protest, brought him into conflict with both his kingly brothers, George IV and William IV. Before his death, he expressed the desire not to be buried at Windsor; his wishes were respected and his remains lie in the public cemetery in Kensal Green.

Holland's speech on 8 April, for all its vigour and display of legal expertise, is interesting for his admission that though in his opinion the treatment of Bonaparte showed 'neither magnanimity nor sound policy', there was a majority 'both in Parliament and out of doors' who thought that detention was necessary. Indiscriminating Bonapartism was represented in fact by a minority lobby or pressure group. The only other noteworthy element of the debate was the speech by Lord Bathurst, Secretary of State for War and the Colonies, who argued, in a show of chauvinistic pride, that though Bonaparte could be considered the prisoner of the allies 'none could keep him with more honour, security and lenity than this country'; in other words, when it came to locking up Corsican usurpers, Britain was best, a sentiment with which most of the population, after twenty-two years of fighting French and Napoleonic ambition, would most likely have agreed.

It was a year later, in March 1817, that Holland returned to the fray. By that time a lot more correspondence, some of it spurious, had passed between London and St Helena. In the latter category was a pamphlet entitled *An Appeal to the British Nation on the Treatment experienced by Napoleon Bonaparte in the island of St Helena*, 'by M. Santini, Porter of the Emperor's Closet'. Among those who accompanied Bonaparte to St Helena, this man is listed variously as usher, barber and occasional tailor. Along with three others of the domestic staff at Longwood, he was expelled by Lowe in 1817 and on reaching England produced the pamphlet. Although it evoked a certain interest, it was soon recognised as a forgery. Bonaparte himself admitted it to be 'a foolish production, exaggerated, full of *coglioniere* (Italian slang meaning balls) and some lies'. At a later period, a certain Colonel Maceroni, who had served under

Murat, confessed that he was the author. He, who had never been to St Helena, says he introduced Santini to Lord Holland and other Bonapartist sympathisers, as a result of which Holland 'moved for papers' in the House of Lords. Ardent though he may have been in defence of Bonaparte's interests, Holland was no fool, so that when he rose to speak in the Lords he based himself not on the so-called Santini brochure but on the Remonstrance, addressed to Lowe by Montholon (but in fact the work of Bonaparte himself). It reached Holland possibly by the hand of Warden, the surgeon on *Northumberland*, who by this time (late summer 1816) had returned to London and had got in touch with Holland. He was invited to dine at Holland House and in the ensuing months, with his insistence on Bonaparte's grievances, became boringly importunate. The Remonstrance was published in London early in 1817 and went through several editions, the fourth of which was reviewed, in highly unfavourable terms, in the *Quarterly*.

Holland knew as well as anyone, and better than most, the reputation of Holland House as an alleged hotbed of Bonapartist intrigue and Foxite gossip. He was therefore at pains to state, in opening his speech in the Lords, that he was not reopening the controversy of a year earlier, on the justice and wisdom of banishing Bonaparte to St Helena. He was not, he said, trying to get the decision reversed, though he still deplored it. Nor was he trying to blame Hudson Lowe, 'the gallant officer who was Governor of St Helena and with many of whose good qualities he had the good fortune to be personally acquainted' (a reference to those dinners at Holland House). He was not such a 'coxcomb' as to suppose that now that Parliament, Ministers and Crown had sanctioned Bonaparte's punishment, he could effect any change in it, 'especially when . . . the opinion of this country went along with Ministers on the subject' – a further admission that Bonapartism in Britain was a minority pursuit.

Having thus cleared the ground, Holland moved on to his principal theme, drawn from the Remonstrance, namely that the captive was being subjected to harsh and unnecessary restrictions. If these reports were false, let them be contradicted; if true, let the faults be corrected. He proceeded to list Bonaparte's grievances, which had to do with his freedom of movement, his freedom to communicate, his freedom to protest, his freedom to receive books and papers, and his financial affairs. What he, Holland, was after were the facts: could the House of Lords be furnished with all the relevant papers, including official correspondence between Lowe and the government and between Bonaparte and London?

Bathurst replied. Like Ministers of all times and of all parties holding office, he was eloquent in rejecting unfavourable or critical allegations about the shortcomings of government policy. He admitted that the Montholon Remonstrance (unlike the so-called Santini brochure) was genuine, but claimed that the complaints arose either from the Governor carrying out his instructions or from a series of misrepresentations, or were 'direct and absolute falsehoods'. He went on to comment on each complaint, arguing that it was either artificial or explaining the reasons for the restriction complained of. One example concerned Bonaparte's house of detention. Arrangements had been set in train for building a new and more commodious dwelling to take the place of Longwood. But when Lowe asked Bonaparte whether he would like a new house or, alternatively, additions to Longwood, there was at first no answer and then an expressed preference for additions, on the grounds that a new house would take five or six years to build, whereas in that time he, Bonaparte, knew 'that in two or three years either the administration [in Britain] would be overturned, or that things would change in France', and 'in either case he should be released'. So Lowe put the Longwood alterations in hand, only to be met with Bonaparte's further objections. Prisoners of war habitually think about their chances of escape or of circumstances somehow changing so that their release becomes a reality, and

Bonaparte was no exception. But in his case the crystal ball was badly clouded.

Read today, Bathurst's speech, though of course it did not satisfy Holland, seems an adequate, even convincing, defence of government policy and a routing of its critics. Perhaps his two strongest debating points were, first, that if heed were to be paid to every complaint from Longwood 'there would be no end of their complaining'. Secondly, that if Bonaparte were to escape, censure would quickly be forthcoming even from those who were arguing for less restraint, and still more strongly from European opinion, which would take the form of suspicions of British connivance. Holland's motion was negatived and without a division. The abiding impressions left from the record of these two debates is that Holland's was a voice, however honourable and courageous, crying in the wilderness. Sympathy with Bonaparte, or any widely backed movement for his release or transfer to some other, less forbidding place of detention, was not there, and no amount of special pleading could arouse it.

Despite his lack of success, Holland considered that his intervention had done some good. Letters to Longwood from members of Bonaparte's family, which had hitherto been held up, were now regularly passed on, and Lord Bathurst's office began to show a more accommodating attitude towards Lady Holland and her wish to supply the captive with clothing, books and other comforts. There is no reason to qualify Holland's description of his wife's feelings about Bonaparte – 'constant, unremitting and unostentatious compassion and generosity'.[11] Bonaparte himself never in his lifetime acknowledged this kindness – Lady Holland never received any letter or communication from him – but other members of his family showed proper gratefulness; his mother, Madame Mère, wrote to Holland from Rome, where she was living, a letter which ended: *'Je suis pour la vie, Milord, votre dévouée servante, la Mère de l'Empereur Napoléon.'*

If Holland managed to derive a certain satisfaction from his efforts on Bonaparte's behalf, the latter took a much more critical stance. His indignation, expressed in a missive that reached Holland in February 1818, was directed not against Holland – that indeed would have been an act of basest ingratitude – but against Bathurst and his speech. The document, about 12,000 words long and entitled 'Observations on Lord Bathurst's speech', was full of strong and bitter refutations of Bathurst's claim that the British government was treating its prisoner with as much generosity as was consistent with security. On the contrary, the true objective of choosing St Helena as a prison, when there was 'no want of castles or houses in England' was to bring about 'a death sufficient slow to be apparently natural'. The 'Observations' were published by the House of Longman and had four editions by the end of 1818.

Over the next five years offerings in profusion went from Holland House to St Helena. Naval ships' captains willingly helped Lady Holland to short-circuit the rule that all communications should go through Bathurst's office. Nor was the infatuated Lady Holland the only benefactor. The Duke of Bedford also sent books, as well as medals that had been specially struck showing Bonaparte's head on one side and the Imperial eagle on the other. The traffic between St Helena and Holland House developed into a two-way stream of people returning, either voluntarily or as deportees, from the Longwood group, most called at Holland House soon after arrival, while others on the way to the island called or got in touch before setting out.

Not everyone who had made the journey to St Helena and back was a Holland House devotee. Admiral Cockburn, the flag officer who had conveyed Bonaparte to the island in *Northumberland*, was back in England by the summer of 1816 and, according to Croker, the First Secretary of the Admiralty, 'gives us no hopes of Bonaparte's dying . . . he eats enormously, but he drinks little, takes regular exercise and in all respects so very careful . . . that he may live 20 years'. Croker was no Bonapartist – his laughter at the Themistocles letter is proof of that. In contrast with this irreverence, Lady Holland, writing in September 1817, considered that:

> the government are displeased that the determination of Napoleon's adherents to continue with him should be known, and more strictness is adopted in the correspondence with the island . . . the impression to be given in this country is that all belonging to him hate and abhor him, and wish to be quit of him; whereas the fact is notoriously the contrary . . . it is rather mortifying to see this country become the jailors [sic] and spies for the Bourbon Government; for to that condition Lord Castlereagh has brought it.

Lady Holland's reference to alleged dissension among the Longwood world is possibly linked with the case of Las Cases. He was the oldest of the group surrounding Bonaparte, and the only one (with the exception of Mme. Bertrand) to speak and understand English. On the voyage to St Helena, and during the year that then elapsed, he was Bonaparte's amanuensis, taking his dictation, which was then fair-copied by Las Cases' fifteen-year-old son. In November 1816 Lowe arrested him and subsequently sent him and his son to the Cape for having tried to smuggle out of the island letters to Europe, which had been written on pieces of silk taffeta and sewn into a waistcoat. An air of mystery hangs over this affair. Another of the Longwood party, O'Meara, the surgeon in *Bellerophon*, who had joined Bonaparte's permanent staff, maintained that it was engineered by Las Cases, who wanted to leave St Helena but did not like to ask Bonaparte for permission to do so. He spent most of 1817 at the Cape and returned to England in November of that year, where he was promptly served with an expulsion order and sent to Belgium; he was again arrested there and moved to Frankfurt, under police supervision. Holland did what he could to help him, although resentful of the way in which he had sought to involve Maitland, a friend of Holland House, in allegations of having set a trap for Napoleon at the time of the latter's surrender. By far the most important help afforded by Holland was to enable Las Cases to repossess his notes, which had been impounded when he was expelled from St Helena. These were vital for him if he were to complete his *Mémoriale de Ste Hélène*, published after Napoleon's death, when it contributed more than any other single source to the birth of the Napoleonic legend.*

As the years of Bonaparte's captivity wore on, the Hollands' interest in and generosity towards him and his little court never flagged. Lady Holland continued to send books (more than a thousand of them over the six years) as well as other comforts, including some jams and preserves; what Bonaparte called '*les pruneaux de Madame Holland*' were almost the last thing he ate.[12] Bertrand, on 29 June 1819, asked Lady Holland, in a letter conveyed secretly, to send 'the new books which are appearing in French, Italian or even English, which might concern us, of travels of discovery in Africa or travel in Europe which look to you as if they ought to interest us'.[13] It was not only non-fiction that was welcome at Longwood. During his first exile at Elba, Bonaparte had shown a liking for English novelists, taking with him books by Maria Edgeworth, Ann Radcliffe and Fanny Burney, as well as William Cobbett's *English Grammar* and a life of Ossian, his favourite poet.[14]

The Duke of Bedford, as already noted, was also a donor, consulting Lady Holland about methods of transmission: 'Have you any means of sending anything to St Helena?'[15] Among his offerings was Robertson's *History of Scotland*, the choice of Lady Holland. Bonaparte, on receiving it, was puzzled: 'Why

---

*Julien Sorel, the hero of Stendhal's novel *Le Rouge et le Noir* (1830) regards Napoleon 'as a god' and the *Mémoriale* as 'the only book in the world, the guide of his life, and object of ecstatic admiration'.

does the Duke of Bedford send me the *History of Scotland*? He must know I have read it.' Then he answered his own question: 'he means to hint to me never to acknowledge, like Mary Queen of Scots, the jurisdiction of England.'[16] Bonaparte was also receiving, presumably through the good offices of Lady Holland, issues of the *Edinburgh Review* and the *Quarterly Review*, and was curious to know how information about his early life had appeared in a particular article: 'Where on earth have they been to hunt out that . . . where on earth could these English Fellows get at it?'[17] Sir Hudson Lowe also supplied Longwood with large quantities of books from the library at Plantation House (the Governor's official residence), as well as newspapers – another indication that Lowe was not the heartless tyrant that Bonaparte made him out to be.

The Longwood group continued to regard Holland House as their surest English source of comfort and help. In January 1820 Countess Montholon, by then back in Europe, wrote from Brussels to Lord Holland: 'It is towards you that justice and misfortune should turn when in need of noble support', she said, and went on to solicit Holland's help in arranging for a suitable replacement at Longwood for her husband, whose poor state of health required his return to Europe; 'the best chance for me is to rely on your intervention'. Holland did not succeed in persuading Bathurst to agree to Mme. Montholon's request. But that did not deter her from returning to the subject ten months later, assuring Holland that she could never sufficiently express her gratitude 'for the interest you are good enough to show towards me, and which I prize highly'. Bertrand, writing after Bonaparte's death (August 1821 – he was himself in London by now, only to find the Hollands absent abroad) speaks of the debt which all 'generous hearts' owe to Holland, as well as 'the gratitude of all the Emperor's friends'.

3

St Helena: The Gaoler and The Gaoled

Once Bonaparte had reached St Helena where he was to spend six years before death ended his detention, he inevitably came into contact with more English people than he had ever encountered in the whole of his life. It was for him a mixed, sometimes a hateful experience,[1] and his hatred centred on one man, the Governor of the island, responsible for carrying out the instructions of the Tory government in London to ensure that the captive did not escape or make unauthorised contact with the outer world. This man's name was Sir Hudson Lowe, whom we have already met dining at Holland House. His reputation as a pettifogging, tactless, suspicious, tyrannical officer, totally unsuitable for the delicate post to which he had been appointed, has ever since been widely accepted, largely as the result of the ceaseless campaign of vilification mounted against him by Bonaparte and his entourage, a campaign since followed up and repeated by many French and some British writers. Among British historians, H.A.L. Fisher possibly achieves the most balanced judgement when he describes Lowe as 'that honourable, pedantic and unfortunate man'.

Born in County Galway in 1769 (which meant that he and Napoleon were within a month of the same age), Lowe spent his infant years in the West Indies, where his father, a regular soldier, was serving with his regiment. On return to England

and while still under the age of twelve, he was appointed ensign in the East Devon militia. By the time he was eighteen, he had obtained a king's commission in the 50th Regiment, his father's unit, and joined it at Gibraltar, where he served for four years. He then took prolonged leave, which he spent travelling in France and Italy, acquiring a thorough knowledge of both languages. After the outbreak of war with France in 1793, Lowe went with his regiment to Corsica to provide part of the garrison at Ajaccio. Disappointingly for lovers of coincidence, he does not appear to have encountered there any members of the Bonaparte family. This was not to be Lowe's only contact with Corsica. A few years later, his regiment was ordered to Minorca, where a number of Corsican émigrés were organised into a small military unit called the Corsican Rangers. Lowe was put in charge of it. The Rangers, with their commander, saw distinguished service in Egypt and were later, after the Peace of Amiens, disbanded, only to be revived a few years after, and once more commanded by Lowe, by now a lieutenant-colonel. The Corsicans' task was to defend the island of Capri. But though Lowe won the praises of his superiors, he was obliged, lacking adequate naval support, to surrender the island to the besieging French. This reverse was partly offset by the Rangers' subsequent success in capturing the neighbouring island of Ischia.

Lowe's connection with these Corsican warriors – which years later at St Helena was to enrage Napoleon – was continued when they formed part of an expedition to drive the French out of the southerly Ionian Islands. The operation was successful, and Lowe was appointed administrator of the islands, a post he held for two years (1810–12). His duties, which made him in effect a species of colonial governor, included contact with the Turkish authorities in Albania, as well as with the Epirot tyrant, Ali Pasha, Byron's admirer.

The much-travelled Lowe now widened his political ex-perience by becoming involved in diplomatic dealings with the King of Sweden and Tsar Alexander, designed to strengthen the anti-Napoleonic alliance. In May 1813, at the hard-fought Battle of Bautzen, east of Dresden, when French forces defeated the combined Russian and Prussian levies, Lowe had his first sight of Napoleon. 'I was on an advanced battery,' he wrote, 'in front of our position and had a most distinct view of him. He was dressed in a plain uniform coat and a star, with a plain hat . . . his air and manner so perfectly resembling [his] portraits, that there was no possibility of mistake.'

Soon after this, Lowe was attached to the Russian-Prussian army, under the command of Field-Marshal Blücher, and was thus present on the field of Leipzig, where Napoleon's crushing defeat marked the beginning of his reversal of fortune. Lowe was with Blücher when the latter crossed the Rhine and remained with the Prussian army, the only British officer to be seconded to Blücher until the capture of Paris. He was the first British officer to bring the news of Napoleon's (first) abdication to London, a mission that earned him a knighthood. During the Hundred Days, as quartermaster-general, he came under the command of the Duke of Wellington, but missed Waterloo by being sent to command a British force in Genoa, which was then deployed in southern France to overcome Bonapartist resistance in Toulon. It was at Marseilles, on 1 August, that Major-General Sir Hudson Lowe received orders to travel forthwith to London, where he would be made Governor of St Helena and entrusted with the custody of the ex-Emperor, by now detained on board HMS *Bellerophon* off Plymouth.

This brief account of Lowe's career up to the moment of his appointment to St Helena suggests a certain pattern: that of a conscientious, loyal, observant officer whose various appointments had given him wide experience not just of the soldier's art but of the ebb and flow of international affairs. In a letter addressed in December 1816 to Lowe from Las Cases, Bonaparte's secretary at St Helena (by this time under arrest for clandestine correspondence), the writer describes the expectations of the French party before the new Governor's arrival:

a man [i.e. Lowe] was appointed to take command here who holds a distinguished rank in the army; he owes his fortune to his personal merit; his life has been passed in diplomatic missions at the headquarters of the Sovereigns of the Continent . . . this man, in his diplomatic career, will have formed just notions both with respect to persons and things. . .

Las Cases quotes Bonaparte himself as having referred to Lowe's battlefield experience, which meant 'that we have then probably exchanged a few cannonballs together and that is always, in my eyes, a noble relation to stand in'. Las Cases' enormously long letter goes on to contrast these expectations with the (alleged) misconduct of Lowe once he had assumed his post.

Why, then, was Lowe's appointment regarded – and not just by Napoleonists – as a disaster? For such was the generally held opinion, at least in retrospect. Sir Walter Scott, a High Tory supporter of the Liverpool government, wrote that strong arguments would be needed 'to induce us to consider him as the very rare and highly exalted species of character to whom . . . this important charge ought to have been entrusted'. Lord Rosebery, in the chapter on Lowe in his St Helena study *The Last Phase*, considered that Lowe's principal defect was 'that he was not what we should call, in the best sense, a gentleman'. The Duke of Wellington identified just the same unhappy defect (and not only in Lowe but also in Napoleon). The Duke had at the time a poor opinion of Lowe, even though later he was to speak up on his behalf: (see Appendix I). 'Sir Hudson Lowe was a very bad choice; he was a man wanting in education and judgement. He was a stupid man, he knew nothing at all of the world and . . . was suspicious and jealous . . . I always thought Lowe was the most unfit person to be charged with the care of Bonaparte's person.'*

*But Wellington also said (autumn 1818) that 'Bonaparte is so damned intractable a fellow there is no knowing how to deal with him' (The Creevey Papers, ed. Sir Herbert Maxwell, 2 vols, London, John Murray 1904).

It was, no doubt, and with hindsight, a pity that Liverpool's government did not consult Wellington before making the St Helena appointment, though it is difficult to imagine that had they done so the Duke's nominee, whoever it might have been, would have escaped the insults and calumnies heaped by Bonaparte and his courtiers on Lowe's head. The insults included calling him a Sicilian hangman ('beja'), a leader of brigands (a reference to the Corsican Rangers), a clerk, and a man 'who had never commanded or been accustomed to, men of honour'. After allowing for Lowe's stiff and somewhat unfortunate manner, and Bonaparte's ceaseless sense of grievance at being locked away on a mid-Atlantic rock, there can be no reasonable doubt about who, had there been a competition for sheer boorishness, would have won it. As one of the courtiers, Count Montholon, told an English friend after Napoleon's death and the return of the Longwood party to Europe, 'an angel from heaven could not have pleased us as Governor of St Helena'.

This point needs to be borne in mind when considering the claim, sometimes made, that Colonel Wilks, whom Lowe succeeded as Governor, would have made a more suitable and acceptable guardian. By all accounts, Wilks was a genial and tactful man. But that did not save him from Bonaparte's irritation, when the departing Wilks went to take leave of him, at the refusal of home-bound British naval and military officers to disregard orders about acting as couriers for Longwood.[2] If Wilks had stayed on, it is more than likely that he would have met with the same opprobrium encountered by Cockburn and Lowe.

Most of the criticism of Lowe, at the time and subsequently, came from allegations by the Longwood group, including the Irish doctor O'Meara. They could not fail to be, in the circumstances, the complete opposite of disinterested parties. Their claims, therefore, need to be put into context. The first and obvious point is that Bonaparte's treatment by his guardian derived from the instructions and directives of Lord Liverpool's government in London. Whether a Whig government would have issued different instructions is a matter for conjecture. What is certain is that those responsible for carrying out the actual policy were its agents, not its authors.

It should not be difficult to enter in the minds of Lord Liverpool and his ministers as they faced the situation in 1815, when Napoleon became their prisoner. Only the most unthinking Napoleonic supporter could try to deny that he had become a standing threat to the peace of Europe. A year earlier, the allied powers thought they had neutralised that threat by dispatching him to Elba, a solution that respected his dignity while clipping his wings – indeed, attempting to remove them altogether. He had escaped, resumed his career as warlord, and finally met defeat on the field of Waterloo. What government in London, of whatever complexion, could do otherwise than to take the most stringent precautions to ensure that this time the cat was well and truly belled?[†]

Napoleon's own idea of living peacefully in the English countryside could never have been (except perhaps to him, though it is hard to think that even he really believed it) anything but laughable. As Thiers, the historian of the Consulate and Empire, was later to write:

> If he had only been a deposed monarch of but ordinary ability, like Louis XVIII, the rules of hospitality would have

---

[†]In February 2001, a military signal book, dating back to the Napoleonic era at St Helena, came to light in the library of Stirling University. It had belonged to Colonal Wilks, the Governor when Bonaparte arrived in the island, and contained flag codes and procedures to be used in the event of any attempt at escape. Among the signals was one which read 'General Bonaparte is missing'. The book is further proof that the government in London, and its agents on the ground, were determined to prevent Bonaparte from repeating his flit from Elba. (report in *The Times*, 28 February 2001)

dictated that Napoleon be allowed to choose, in the freedom of England, a place where he could have ended his days. But to permit a man who had escaped from Elba, and drawn the arms of Europe on to the fields of Ligny and Waterloo, to roam the streets of London was out of the question.[3]

St Helena was admittedly a desolate and unappealing spot. It was chosen precisely for those reasons – although Wellington, on the basis of a fortnight's stay many years before, blithely maintained that it was a very pleasing place with a charming climate.

The location of the prison once chosen, the rules of imprisonment had to be drawn up. It was here that the most vehement critics of the system found their voice, both at the time (Holland and his friends) and later (Rosebery and countless French writers, including Thiers, who thought that 'detaining Napoleon did not confer the right to torment, nor to shorten his life, nor, above all, to humiliate him . . . to respect his genius was a duty as important as the right to restrain him'). Respecting genius is one thing; failing to take every possible precaution to prevent one's prisoner from escaping is another. The instructions issued by Bathurst to Cockburn before *Northumberland* sailed for St Helena have already been described (see Chapter 2, p. 45). In the light of the prevailing circumstances, there seems nothing in these instructions to constitute torment or humiliation.

It is always possible, of course, that a more enlightened, magnanimous or simply practical-minded authority in London – and Bathurst was short of all these qualities – would have devised a less oppressive regime. Wellington certainly thought so. He would have let Bonaparte wander about on the island wherever he liked and speak to whomever he wished, on the strict condition that he showed himself to a British officer every night and morning. The trouble with this is that not only did Wellington advise such a scheme twenty-seven years after Bonaparte was first banished to St Helena (he spoke of it to Stanhope on 21 December 1848)[4] when hindsight came easily, but also there is no guarantee that Wellington's rules would have silenced the complaints of the Longwood party, above all those of its principal member. And would the latter's pathological hatred of Lowe have been to any degree mitigated? It seems to me extremely doubtful that even if, to use Montholon's graphic analogy, Lowe's place had been taken by an angel, the St Helena story would have read very, or at all, differently.

One instruction, however, had a constant and predictable effect. This was that the captive was never to be addressed, verbally or in writing, as Emperor. His rank and status were defined as those of a retired general officer, which is what he undoubtedly was. It is not clear who, in London, was responsible for this ruling, which began to be enforced when he first boarded *Bellerophon*. It appears to have been founded on the fact that the British government, unlike the governments of Russia, Austria or Prussia, had never recognised Napoleon's self-proclaimed status as Emperor, though it had recognised him as First Consul. There was therefore no need to do so now that he had been defeated and made, in effect, a prisoner of war. Moreover, Britain, as a supporter of the restored Bourbon dynasty, could not logically think or speak in terms of two French sovereigns. If Louis XVIII was the legitimate King of France, what was Bonaparte Emperor of? He had been allowed to keep the title of Emperor at Elba,[5] however ridiculous that was, but now there was no Elba, only a lonely outpost with its British Governor.

Whatever the worth of these arguments, it was a childish instruction, of dubious or non-existent advantage to anyone or any cause. But there it was, and Lowe was bound to observe it, which he did, it must be said, with relentless zeal. At least he did not make such an egregious ass of himself in this respect as Admiral Cockburn, who had brought Bonaparte to St Helena in *Northumberland* and who remained responsible for his custody until Lowe arrived to take up his duties as Governor. In reply to a vigorous protest from Montholon (dictated or at least inspired, like most of the communications from Longwood, by Bonaparte himself) in which there were frequent references to 'the Emperor' and 'his Majesty', Cockburn replied that, 'I have no cognizance of such a person'. He repeated this piece of black comedy a short time later when Bertrand asked him to forward, unopened, a sealed letter from the 'Emperor' to the Prince Regent. Cockburn's response was that 'I have no knowledge of the person designated by you, "the Emperor", there being no person on this island I consider entitled to such a dignity'. Like Lowe after him, Cockburn was bound to carry out his instructions, but it was maladroit and unnecessary to do so with quite such punctiliousness. On one occasion, Bonaparte, instead of his habitual outbursts of indignation, tried a little humour. The Admiral invited him to a ball, inevitably addressing the missive to General Bonaparte. The latter told Montholon to 'send this card to General Bonaparte. The last I heard of him was at the pyramids or Mount Thabor'.[6]

But this comparatively good-natured irony could and did not alter the prescribed procedure. The Admiral refused to forward the sealed letter, quoting his instructions that letters to and from Longwood must first be read by Admiral or Governor. Lowe in his turn was to enforce the same system. Placed as he was, he could not do otherwise. The Longwood group naturally did not see things in that light. But it is an important point, when considering the guilty verdict that so many chroniclers have passed on Lowe, to realise that Bonaparte and his companions were just as indignant about their treatment at the hands of Cockburn as later they were about Lowe. They liked to pretend – they had almost certainly come to believe it – that times had been better under Cockburn. In fact, there was little if any difference in the rules governing Bonaparte's detention between Cockburn's and Lowe's application of those rules.

Further evidence that the captive was actually looking forward with pleasure to Lowe's arrival comes from O'Meara, the surgeon in *Northumberland*, who on arrival became, at Bonaparte's request, his personal physician, and from Sir George Bingham, commander of the island's garrison. The former wrote to a friend at the Admiralty in London in April 1816 that 'Lowe had taken charge of Napoleon out of the hands of Sir George Cockburn, very much to the satisfaction of both Napoleon and Sir George himself'. Bingham, in a letter to Lowe some years later, 'distinctly' recalled[7] that Bonaparte's first reaction had been friendly. On being told by Bingham that the ship bearing Lowe had been sighted, he said, 'I am glad of it. I am tired of the Admiral, and there are many points I should like to talk over with Sir Hudson Lowe. He has been a soldier and has served. He was with Blücher; besides, he commanded the Corsican regiment and knows many of my friends and acquaintances'. This last statement (assuming that Bingham reported it correctly: his French was poor, his Italian non-existent) reads strangely, in the light of Bonaparte's later ful-minations about Lowe's connections with the Rangers.

Bonaparte and Lowe faced each other only six times, all of them within the first few months of Lowe's governorship. Anyone trying to give an account of what passed at these meetings must inevitably draw, anyway for one side of the picture, on Lowe's reports. As might be expected, these differ significantly, sometimes fundamentally, from the descriptions of the same occasions in the diaries or writings of Montholon, Las Cases or O'Meara. The important point here is that none of these was present when Lowe was talking with Bonaparte. The Longwood scribes must all have based their reports on what he, Bonaparte, subsequently told them. Not only, as we have seen, had he devised a long-term strategy for discrediting Lowe, but his reputation for not telling the truth when it suited him was so well known that his value as a witness or reporter of events at which he was present must be rated as very low indeed or even discounted altogether. Of course, Lowe, for his part, was intent on justifying himself – to Bathurst or perhaps to posterity, if his prosaic mind ever dwelt on such a distant and hazy prospect. But it is impossible to resist the conclusion that Lowe's testimony and reporting ability are more to be trusted than the accounts related to his entourage by the permanently aggrieved, mendacious and revengeful ex-Emperor.

The first projected meeting between the two men never took place. On 16 April 1816, only two days after his arrival from England, Lowe went to Longwood to pay his respects but arrived too early for 'the Emperor' and had to return on the following afternoon, accompanied by Cockburn. Whether by design or accident, Cockburn was not admitted to the inner room where Bonaparte was waiting, so that Lowe and his prisoner were alone. The contretemps seems to have been caused by an over-zealous servant.

Whoever or whatever was responsible for the failure to admit Cockburn, Bonaparte, according to Las Cases, was elated by what had happened: 'he [burst] into a fit of laughter and exhibited the joy of a child.' He did have the good grace to send Montholon to apologise to Cockburn. But in private, to his courtiers he said that if the Admiral had entered, 'I should without hesitation have apostrophised him in the presence of his countryman. I should have told him that by the same sentiment attached to the honourable uniform which we had both worn for forty years, I accused him of having, in the eyes of the world, degraded his nation and his sovereign by wantonly and stupidly failing in respect to one of the oldest soldiers in Europe'. Here is further proof that Bonaparte's animosity towards Cockburn, whatever comparisons he might later come to make between the Admiral and Lowe, was just as pronounced as his feelings about the Governor.

This first meeting seems, from Lowe's record, to have been without incident. The conversation took place in Italian, which appears to have been Bonaparte's preferred language. His spoken French could be difficult to follow, especially for a foreigner. Lady Malcolm, wife of the Admiral who succeeded

Cockburn, described him in her diary as speaking 'thick and quick', and she did not get all the words.[8]

According to form, Bonaparte did most of the talking, dwelling at some length on his Egyptian campaign, presaging in one remark the idea of the Suez Canal.[‡] On learning that Lowe was married, he said, 'Ah, you have your wife with you, you are well off'. When Lowe told him that he had been twenty-eight years a soldier, Bonaparte replied, 'I am therefore an older soldier than you'. Lowe then asked permission to present Sir Thomas Reade, his principal subordinate, and Major Gorrequer, his private secretary. O'Meara, in the same letter to his friend in London already quoted, wrote that 'this new Governor is a man of very few words but he appears to be a polite man'. O'Meara goes on to describe his conversation with Bonaparte after the Lowe visit, when the latter inveighed against Cockburn, particularly for his behaviour in *Northumberland* on the voyage out. 'Not wishing', he said, 'to sit at table for two or three hours like the English, guzzling down wine to make myself drunk', he left the table and walked out, whereupon Cockburn said, 'in a contemptuous manner', that he believes the General 'has never read Lord Chesterfield', meaning that 'I was deficient in politeness and did not know how to sit at table . . . this was a most gross insult to me'. The story contrasts sharply with the accounts of deference shown to him in *Bellerophon*, suggesting that the atmosphere in *Northumberland* may not have been quite as pleasant as at first supposed.

[‡]This was not as visionary as it might appear. The idea of linking the Mediterranean with the Red Sea goes back as far as the 26th Pharaonic dynasty (end of the 7th century B.C.) and was re-conceived in the early Muslim period in Egypt (7th to 8th century A.D.). But the idea did not take practical form until, in the middle of the 19th century, Ferdinand de Lesseps began superintending the 10-year task of cutting a canal across the narrow isthmus of Suez.

Longwood[9] was a large converted farmhouse, standing on a high plateau (1,600 feet above sea-level), which in bad winter weather was windswept and cold. By the time Cockburn's alterations and additions had made the place ready for occupation, it consisted of some thirty-six rooms, including servants' quarters. The largest, made of wood, was the so-called billiard room, first used as a dining room until Lowe caused a billiard table to be installed. Here Bonaparte would spend much of his time, walking up and down dictating. For his personal use, he had two small (15- by 14-foot) rooms, one a study (it later became the bedroom), the other the bedroom, where Cockburn had a fireplace built. It was because of this fireplace that Bonaparte later used the room as a study. A door led from it into the adjoining bathroom.

Elsewhere in this sprawling, low-built structure was a good-sized dining room, though because it was an interior room it had no windows; the salon, where Bonaparte would receive his visitors and where, his bed having been moved, he died; and a library. All the rooms, except the billiard room, were built without cellars or under-floor ventilation. This meant that the house was perpetually damp, as well as being hot in summer and cold in winter, especially in its back, southern quarters, where Cockburn had run up a number of wooden rooms to accommodate Las Cases and his son, Gourgaud, and the Montholon family.

It was very far from being a palace, which explains why at some point Bonaparte suggested that he and his staff should take over Plantation House, the Governor's official residence. Lowe was sympathetically aware of Longwood's shortcomings. He reported that the house and its furnishings were inadequate for 'what might be considered to appertain to a General Officer of any rank in any other place – very inferior indeed, to that of the house allotted to me'.

While this was proof that, despite his legendary reputation as an unthinking martinet, Lowe in fact had the interests of his unhappy French prisoners at heart, it did not mean that he was ready to vacate his own comfortable dwelling. 'I do not want to hand over Plantation House to the French – they would do too much damage there, and besides Lady Lowe would not be so well at Longwood, and I will never sacrifice my Wife's health to Bonaparte's comfort.'[§]

The only solution was to build another house for the French party, but before that something more immediate had to be done. At the end of April 1816, hearing that Bonaparte was unwell, Lowe went to see him (their second meeting) and suggested that he should call on the advice of an English doctor in government employ – Dr Baxter – to add to that of O'Meara. Bonaparte would not hear of it: 'I want no doctors.' Until the last months of his life, when mortal illness closed in on him, he steadfastly refused the services of any doctor suggested by or answering to the Governor.

This second conversation with Lowe on 30 April, when French seems to have been the language, Bonaparte embarked on a long series of complaints, though they were directed not so much at Lowe personally as at the British government. He regretted giving himself up to the British, he found St Helena detestable and Longwood particularly so. When Lowe said that better furniture and comforts were on the way, he replied, melodramatically, 'Let them send me a coffin; a couple of balls in the head is all that is necessary. What does it signify if I lie on

---

[§]The memory of Longwood's rigours lived on into modern times. In January 1946 General de Gaulle, disillusioned with the direction French post-war politics were taking, resigned as head of the provisional government and retreated to a government-owned property, a former royal hunting lodge, at Marly, near Paris. Two days after the move, seated on a packing-case full of his papers and documents, he told a visiting reporter, '*Ici, c'est Longwood*' (*The Locust Years: The story of the Fourth French Republic*, by Frank Giles, London, Secker and Warburg, 1991, p. 26).

a velvet couch or a fustian? I have been landed here like a convict. . .'

Months before setting eyes on Lowe, the man for whom he was to conceive such an implacable loathing, Bonaparte had made an English contact which brought him real pleasure and relatively the happiest period, brief though it was, of his entire St Helena existence. This was the Balcombe family. William Balcombe was an employee of the East India Company and general purveyor, who lived in an attractive little property, The Briars, not far from Longwood House. Bonaparte spent his first two months on the island here, while Longwood, previously the hot-weather residence of the lieutenant-governor, was being prepared. There were two young daughters of the family, both of whom spoke French well enough to make possible converse with their visitor. He was especially taken with Betsy, the younger, high-spirited, something of a tomboy, who treated Bonaparte with a lack of respect that shocked the French courtiers – boxing his ears, pretending to attack him with his own sword. Bonaparte revenged himself by running away with her ball dress, and they both played at blind man's buff. She was allowed to interrupt him – or anyway did interrupt – whenever she chose, even during the afternoon siesta, and more than once burst in when he was dictating to Las Cases. The ex-Emperor, who was good with children, was obviously amused, although he finally wearied of the family, denouncing them as '*canaille*', a favourite word when he wanted to denigrate a person or persons.

Betsy later married a Mr Abell and wrote a book about her recollections of Bonaparte.[10] Like so many memoirs of this genre, her stories must be suspected of embellishment, but there can be little doubt that for a time something akin to a flirtation prevailed between the bouncy young girl and the temporarily ebullient captive. Balcombe himself, who returned with his family to England early in 1818, seems to have been won over (possibly with French money) to the Bonapartist cause and almost certainly provided one of the channels through which forbidden correspondence reached the outer world. Despite these supposed sympathies, Balcombe figured among those who were ready to testify in Lowe's favour when, years later, the latter was preparing to bring a case of libel against O'Meara.

On 17 May 1816, at the third meeting between the Governor and his prisoner, all pretence at civility on the part of Bonaparte evaporated and Lowe was treated to an exhibition of temper and personal hostility such that, as he subsequently reported to Bathurst, 'I feel it more and more difficult to reconcile the exercise of my duty with the high respect, regard and attention which he seems to require'. He must indeed have been sorely tried by Bonaparte's outbursts – 'such rapidity, such intemperance, and so much warmth that it is difficult to repeat every word he used'. But though Lowe's predicament commands sympathy, he had partly brought it on himself, in a manner that goes some way to justify the Duke of Wellington's apparently condescending complaint that he knew nothing about the world.

A week previously, the Countess of Loudon and Moira, wife of Earl Moira, Governor-General of India, had arrived at St Helena en route to England. Lowe had the doubtless well-intentioned but obviously ill-conceived idea of inviting Bonaparte to dinner to meet her. (One can visualise the scene as it might have occurred: the drawing room at Government House, the ladies in their best dresses, the men mostly in uniform with decorations. 'Allow me, madam, to present to you General Bonaparte, one of our neighbours here, of whom you will probably have heard.') The invitation, addressed to 'General Bonaparte', went to Bertrand, the Grand Marshal, but there was no answer except for a courteous message to Lady Loudon saying that he, Bonaparte, would have been charmed to pay his respects if she had been within his limits, and he sent some sweets for her children. The reference to limits reveals one of Bonaparte's main grievances.

These limits, within which he was free to walk or ride unescorted, were laid down from the beginning. Lowe did not invent them, though he did amend them. The 'free' area consisted of a circuit of twelve miles surrounding Longwood.#
Beyond this area, Bonaparte would have to be escorted by a British officer, a condition that Bonaparte consistently and vehemently refused to accept. Going to dinner at Plantation House (on the supremely unlikely assumption that he would ever have been ready to do so) would have meant going beyond the twelve-mile limit and therefore an escort would have been required. After the invitation went unanswered, Lowe told Bertrand that he himself, the Governor, would with pleasure have escorted Bonaparte to Plantation House, or sent a member of his personal staff.

But Bertrand predictably replied that his master would never go beyond the twelve-mile radius if it meant that an officer had to go with him. There the matter of dinner at the Governor's came to an end. But Lowe's thick skin remained unaffected, at least on this point. Only three months later he was asking Bertrand to invite 'the Emperor' (he did not of course call him that) to attend the official annual party to mark the Prince Regent's birthday.[11] He had accepted a similar invitation at Elba (see p. 14), but now very different circumstances prevailed. Lady Lowe, who sounds as though she had more savoir-faire

---

#One one occasion, in January 1816, Bonaparte and his companions Gourgaud and Las Cases had a potentially lethal encounter with British regulations. Out riding, they were challenged by a sentry. Gourgaud said he would remain to reason with the man, while Bonaparte and Las Cases rode on at a gallop. The sentry loaded and cocked his rifle and would have given chase, but Gourgaud stopped him. It was all a mistake; the Frenchmen were not beyond the limits. Bonaparte commented that 'poor Las Cases thought he would get a bullet in the back'.

than her husband, predicted that Bonaparte 'would not come to my house, and I thought him perfectly right'.

The affair of the dinner invitation was not allowed to be forgotten at Longwood. In the long letter from Las Cases to Lowe, already quoted, he is clearly outraged at the very idea. 'Had you thought what you were doing? Did you suppose that acceptance was possible? And in what an embarrassing position such acceptance would have put you? Would you have addressed your guest as General? [The answer must be yes.] And what sort of a General – a divisional General or a General-in-Chief? Where would you have seated him?'

The importance of *place à table*, which to this day gives Paris hostesses more grounds for anxiety and, on the part of their guests, possible offended feelings than the quality of the food and wine, had already caused trouble at St Helena. In November 1815, a few weeks after Bonaparte's arrival, Cockburn's ball (see p. 69) was attended by several of the Longwood party. Most of them enjoyed themselves, particularly Mme. de Montholon, and even the prickly Las Cases had no complaint. But Gourgaud refused to sit in the place allotted to him.

Shortly afterwards, he again, and with rather more reason, considered himself insulted, when at a luncheon given by Sir George Bingham he found rather than being wrongly placed, there was no place laid for him at all. When informed of these lapses in protocol, Napoleon was furious, particularly over Mrs Wilks, the Governor's wife, being given precedence, at Cockburn's ball, over Mme Bertrand, 'a real lady, instead of Mrs Wilks, who is only the wife of a petty Governor'.[12]

'Sir,' said Las Cases in his protest to Lowe, 'each plan, each word, each step is an outrage: and to whom would you have addressed them? To perhaps the proudest soul in the universe. I must tell you, in translating this note [the invitation] I went pale with surprise and indignation.' In his written notes on Las Cases' letter, Lowe says he regrets having issued the invitation.

Napoleon being rowed to HMS *Bellerophon*, off Rochefort, 1815. From an aquatint by Jazet.

Bellerophon at Plymouth, with Bonaparte on board, surrounded by
boatloads of sightseers. One of J.M.W. Turner's illustrations for
Scott's *Life of Napoleon*. See page 142.

Bonaparte on *Bellerophon* from the painting by
Sir Charles Eastlake. See page 21.

Napoleon on board *Bellerophon*. From a painting by Sir W.Q. Orchardson. Executed in 1909.

Bonaparte's dinner table in HMS *Northumberland*, en route for St Helena.

View of Longwood, Bonaparte's place of detention at St Helena.

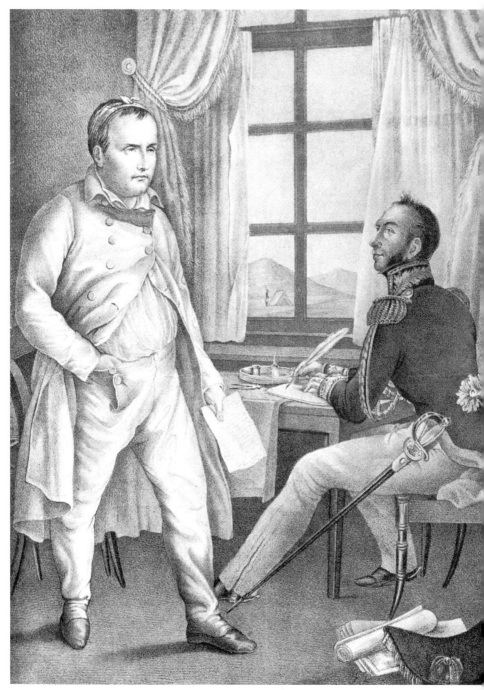

Bonaparte at St Helena, dictating to Gourgaud. From a lithograph by Steuben.

Lieut-General Sir Hudson Lowe.
From a pencil sketch,
probably by Abraham Wivell.

*Two contrasting images of
Bonaparte's 'gaoler'*

rench version of the same.
n a drawing by J.N. Frémy,
raved by J.M. Fontaine.
page 85.

Bonaparte in the garden
at Longwood.

Bonaparte undoing cases of books, many of them sent by Lady Holland.

Well he might. If Las Cases could work himself up in this way, seven months after Lowe perpetrated his gaffe, there should have been little surprise at the explosion of the notoriously irascible Bonaparte when Lowe visited him on 17 May, within a week of the offence. He began by telling the prisoner of the plans for a new and more comfortable house for him, or alternatively for the addition of two or three rooms to Longwood. Bonaparte, 'standing with his hat under his arm, in the manner he usually presents himself when he assumes his imperial dignity [Lowe's report]', maintained a stony silence until he finally burst out:

> I cannot understand the conduct of your government towards me. Do they want to kill me? Are you come here to be my executioner, my gaoler? . . . when I heard of your arrival in this island, I thought that, as an officer of the army, I should find you possessed of politer manners than the Admiral [Cockburn] who, as a naval officer, might have had a rougher bearing. I have no fault to find with his heart. But how do you treat me? It is an insult to invite me to dinner and to call me General Bonaparte. I am the Emperor Napoleon. Are you come here to be my executioner, my gaoler?

The tirade flowed on without cease and without Lowe attempting to stop it. When, presumably for want of breath, it died away, Lowe said – and who can reasonably blame him? – 'Sir, I have not come here to be insulted . . . if you are not disposed to speak about [the question of accommodation] I will retire'. Bonaparte evidently felt some remorse, saying that he did not mean to insult the Governor, but 'how have you treated me? Has it been in a way becoming to a soldier?' With commendable dignity, considering the provocation, Lowe explained that 'I am a soldier to perform the duties I owe to my country in conformity with its customs'.

But this mollified the angry Corsican only briefly. He was soon back on the rant, alleging in his fury that Lowe 'had received orders to kill me – yes, to kill me. Yes, Sir, you have received orders to do any and everything', a charge to which Lowe responded, again with restraint, by reminding Bonaparte that at their previous meeting he, Bonaparte, had admitted that he had misunderstood the character of the English people, 'and you now equally misunderstand that of the English soldier'. In reporting this stormy clash to Bathurst, Lowe said – and there is no evidence to the contrary – that he had kept calm: 'General Bonaparte's anger drew forth no violence of language or expression from me.'

It should be clear from the intemperate nature of Bonaparte's attitude that more than the tactless invitation to dinner was involved. It was now seven months since he had arrived on the island, and not a glimmer of hope had yet shown itself that he might be transferred to a less inhospitable prison, or even that conditions of his captivity might be relaxed. He seems to have believed that the Prince Regent's daughter, Princess Charlotte, was favourable to his cause, and that were she to come to the throne, his prospects might improve. Princess Caroline, the Regent's estranged wife and mother of Princess Charlotte, whose claims the Whigs supported as a way of getting at the unpopular Regent, was an admirer of Bonaparte, and the latter evidently supposed, or at least hoped, that the mother would influence the daughter. But that was a distant hope in 1816, when the Regent was not yet king. Angry and pining in his lonely prison, he convinced himself that had he been able to get to London and been in touch with Ministers and MPs he could have influenced them: 'my logic would have won over men like Grey and Grenville [two prominent Whigs, the latter Prime Minister briefly in 1806].' Meanwhile he felt free to paint Lowe in colours as repellent as possible. 'I can do as I like with the Governor's reputation, all that I can say about him, about his bad treatment and his ideas of poisoning me, will be believed.'[13] In other words, his behaviour towards and charges against Lowe were dictated as much by political reasons as by genuine grievances, although there were of course plenty of those.

But however bitter he felt about his fate, however resolved to squeeze the last drops of propaganda out of the situation, Bonaparte could still experience remorse about his campaign against Lowe. Las Cases, in his journal entry for 31 May 1816, a fortnight after the wrathful meeting just described, records Bonaparte saying

> I behaved very ill to him, no doubt, and nothing but my present situation could excuse me; but I was out of humour and could not help it. Had such a scene taken place at the Tuileries I should have felt myself bound in conscience to make some atonement . . . but here I uttered not a syllable of conciliation and I had no wish to do so. However, the Governor proved himself very insensible to my severity; his delicacy did not seem wounded by it. I should have liked, for his sake, to have seen him evince a little anger, or pull the door violently after him . . . it would at least have shown that there was some spring and elasticity about him, but I found nothing of the kind.

There could be no better illumination of the chasm separating the personality of the defeated Emperor, a Mediterranean genius prone to sudden, hot-blooded rages and outbursts, and the stiff, self-controlled British officer who was in effect his gaoler.

There were three further meetings between the Governor and the captive. On 17 July 1816, in the course of a long conversation, Bonaparte gave vent to a whole series of complaints about the way he was being treated, comparing Lowe's regime unfavourably with that of Cockburn. Lowe countered with the usual argument that he was only carrying out his instructions. As to a new house, the matter Lowe had come to discuss, Bonaparte said it would take six years to build, whereas 'in a couple of years there will be a change in the Ministry in England and I shall no longer be here'. Reporting this conversation to Bathurst, Lowe had some grievances of his own: 'I have been myself more unjustly and harshly treated by him in more than one instance . . . I have abstained from any possible

81

act or expression which I thought could give offence and my sins towards him have been solely those of having executed my instructions.'

This had clearly been an unpleasant meeting, not as acrimonious as the previous one, but a good deal more tolerable than the sixth and final encounter between the two men – final because after that Bonaparte refused any longer to receive him. This cannot have been much hardship to Lowe, for whom these bruising contacts must have been a repeated trial. But it meant that formal relations between the prisoner and Plantation House had from then on to be handled by Sir Thomas Reade, Lowe's Chief of Staff, a man towards whom Bonaparte showed less hostility.

But before the irretrievable break, there was the fifth round in the Lowe–Bonaparte contest, and this saw Bonaparte back on his best behaviour. It took place on 21 June, when the Governor went to Longwood to present the newly arrived Rear-Admiral Sir Pulteney Malcolm, successor to Sir George Cockburn as naval commander at St Helena and the Cape of Good Hope. By the same frigate as brought the Admiral came two handsome volumes, the work of John Cam Hobhouse, by now Lord Broughton, Byron's friend and a passionate admirer of 'the Emperor'. The books, containing Hobhouse's recollections of being in Paris in 1814–15, were intended as a present for Bonaparte. But he had written in one of them 'Imperatori Napoleon' and that was sufficient for Lowe to withhold them from Longwood. He was doubtless emboldened in this action by Hobhouse's courteous letter, authorising him, if it seemed improper to forward them to Bonaparte, to place them in his own library. Given the 'no-Emperor' rule, Lowe was only being logical and consistent. From this distance, it seems a petty way to behave, but Lowe, full of integrity and devotion to duty, had the mind of an unimaginative bureaucrat.

Bonaparte could have known nothing of this when he received the Governor and the Admiral. No matters of substance were discussed, but Bonaparte, according to Lowe's dispatch to Bathurst in London,[14] 'addressed to me several polite and attentive inquiries respecting myself and Lady Lowe'. The Admiral, who presumably had been briefed by Lowe about Bonaparte's previous behaviour, thought that this improvement in manners showed a 'very marked overture'. In light of the way in which, in the succeeding months, Bonaparte sought to keep his relationship with the Admiral, and especially with Lady Malcolm, on a friendly and agreeable footing, in contrast with his conduct towards Lowe, it seems highly probable that at this first encounter with the Admiral he set out with the express purpose of impressing Malcolm by representing himself as a well-mannered, reasonable human being. There is massive testimony, throughout his career, that when he chose to use charm he could exert it as easily as he could fall into one of his rages.

Less than a month later, on 18 August, the temperature between the Governor and his prisoner once more descended to sub-zero. This was to be the last meeting between the two men and it was one of the longest and most unremittingly fractious. It began with Lowe trying to get from Bonaparte, not for the first time, some indications of his wishes about improvements to Longwood, only to be met with a rehearsal of past grievances about the treatment and restraints imposed. Lowe replied, as so often before, that he was only doing his dutiful best, to which Bonaparte reported that 'in your correspondence you pay us compliments and at the same time you are sticking pins into us'. What he was referring to was the right of Longwood in-habitants to exchange letters with other citizens of St Helena, which Lowe would not allow. This had, just previously, brought about a sharp exchange of letters between Bertrand and Lowe. Bonaparte now accused the Governor of having insulted the Grand Marshal and said that Bertrand ought to have cut Lowe's throat. The latter pointed out that Bertrand had accused him of 'abuse of power and injustice' and said that he 'was no more formed to be a tyrant in practice than a slave in thought'.

Bonaparte changed tack to make other complaints and harked back to the (alleged) difference of Cockburn's regime compared with Lowe's: 'you are a Lieutenant-General and should not perform your duty like a sentinel.' Lowe replied that he was there to do his duty, 'which I esteem above glory'. And so the circular and repetitive arguments went on, to the mutual dissatisfaction of both parties. Lady Malcolm, in her diary (see p. 99), gives a longer account of this meeting, at which Admiral Malcolm was also present.

According to this, Lowe's main purpose was to complain of Bertrand's improper conduct towards him as Governor. Bonaparte was having none of this. Bertrand, he said, had commanded armies (untrue – he was an engineer officer) and 'he [nodding towards Lowe] treats him like a corporal'. Then, turning to Lowe, he burst out 'you vex us hourly, by your little ways, you do not know how to conduct yourself towards men of honour, your soul is too low . . . you treat us like Botany Bay convicts, you are not a General, you are only a scribe of office'. The insulted Lowe soon bade his captive good morning, followed by the Admiral, who recorded, via his wife's diary, that Lowe – 'never for a moment lost his temper, Bonaparte frequently'.[15]

A short time after this, Sir Thomas Reade reported a conversation he had had with Las Cases. The latter said that 'The Emperor was sorry he had lost his temper so much in the last interview with the Governor, that all the time he had been on the throne of France he had never been in such a passion and that he had lowered himself by it'.[16] Remorse was evidently a frequent emotion with this unhappy man.

A French phrase, '*dialogue des sourds*', describes a conversation between two mutually incompatible people, neither ready for a second to agree with what the other is propounding. It is not a question, as the French words might suggest, literally of not hearing, but of total rejection of what the other is saying, even before he has said it. Lowe heard and understood all right

84

– he could not avoid doing so – what Bonaparte was saying. With much of it – that exile to St Helena was a disagreeable fate, that Longwood was uncomfortable, that it was irksome to have a British officer always hanging about – he was in no valid position to disagree, nor did he try to do so. When he could get a word in, it was usually to point out that he was only carrying out his instructions, not a response likely to comfort the embittered captive. But the Governor did sympathise openly with some of the complaints and offered to do what he could to remedy them – in the case of Longwood by building a new house or improving the existing one. Bonaparte would have none of it; he seemed in a way to glory in his discomfort, as a fanatical martyr at the stake welcomes the flames that are consuming him. The important thing was that the outer world should learn of his plight, which explains why the Longwood tenants spent so much of their time and energy devising means of smuggling out correspondence.

Many contemporary accounts, not all of them French-inspired, speak of Lowe's unprepossessing appearance and manner. Portraits of him are of little help. One, reproduced as the frontispiece of the three volumes by William Forsyth, Lowe's principal apologist, reveals a benign figure, the countenance open, the eyes well set apart and almost twinkling with incipient good humour, the arms folded to give a feeling of friendly informality. It is possibly by Abraham Wivell (1786–1849) who specialised in small, highly-finished drawings. Another, drawn by the French artist J.N. Frémy, shows a stern, near-cadaverous face, with close-set and unsmiling eyes, the very image of a military martinet.* That he could be tactless and insensitive there is no doubt, as these pages attest. It is arguable that a more secure and sophisticated a man – what

---

*The British Library possesses copies of both engravings. It is difficult to avoid the suspicion that Frémy was painting to order, the order being to make Lowe look as disagreeable as possible.

Rosebery would have called 'a gentleman' – would have handled the situation better and thus avoided the contumely that so many writers have heaped on Lowe. I doubt this. The inescapable facts are that Lowe, with all his character defects, was bound to carry out his instructions to prevent any possibility of Bonaparte escaping, while the latter and his followers were convinced not only that they were being subjected to cruel and unnecessary repression but that their very banishment to St Helena was a monstrous breach of international practice. There could not be, and there was not, any building of bridges here.

The Englishman with whom Bonaparte in 1816 and 1817 had had the most sustained contact, indeed the Englishman whom he got to know and like better than any other, was O'Meara – except that, as his name suggests, he was not English but Irish. Born in Ireland in 1786, Barry Edward O'Meara first served as a medical officer in the army and then transferred to the Royal Navy, serving as a surgeon in various warships. In that capacity he was part of the *Bellerophon's* ship's company when Napoleon surrendered. Maitland had a high opinion of him. As the French doctor detailed to accompany Napoleon to St Helena withdrew from the mission, the ex-Emperor, who had taken a liking to O'Meara – he spoke decent French and Italian – asked him to fill the vacant place. So from October 1815 onwards this cheerful, likeable and talented young doctor lived at Longwood and had frequent, often daily, contact with Bonaparte, who talked freely to him. O'Meara certainly did not begin as a Bonapartist; indeed, he refused the salary offered by Bonaparte, preferring to retain his independence by remaining on the Royal Naval pay list, an arrangement agreed to by the Admiralty.

Whether he realised it fully or not, he was bound to find himself in an increasingly anomalous situation, subject to opposing pressures and conflicts of loyalties. As the only inmate of Longwood free to come and go as he pleased, he was regarded by the French as a useful intermediary, someone who could liaise with visiting ships, bring them news and newspapers, and convey forbidden missives and messages. On the other hand, as a serving British officer, the only non-Frenchman permanently at Longwood, he was required to report to Lowe the details of his conversations with Bonaparte and also deliver messages to the French courtiers. He was thus in the position of a double agent who in the end was virtually bound to displease one or other of his patrons, perhaps both. And he was not only reporting to Lowe. He also wrote long (and fascinating) letters about what he had seen and heard to his friend at the Admiralty in London, a Mr Finlaison.[tt] The latter in turn passed them on to Croker, Secretary to the Admiralty, who circulated copies to members of the Cabinet. They seem to have been shown also to the Prince Regent, judging from what Finlaison told O'Meara in a letter[17] acknowledging receipt of the St Helena missive: 'your letters . . . furnished a real feast to very great folks here . . . I conjecture [they] have even amused His Royal Highness the Prince Regent.'

But already O'Meara was storing up trouble for himself. In June 1816 a British warship arrived at Portsmouth from St Helena, and shortly after a Portsmouth newspaper printed an account of Longwood and its inhabitants. Suspicion turned on O'Meara, and Bathurst wrote to Lowe[18] that 'it will not be prudent to place any confidence in Dr. O'Meara', adding that it might be necessary to remove him from the island. O'Meara, taxed by Lowe with misconduct, denied having anything to do with the Portsmouth business. But there is no doubt that the French did use him as a conduit. He himself admitted that Montholon had tried (unsuccessfully, he said) to persuade him

[tt]These enormously long and detailed letters, which must have taken O'Meara hours to write, are bound up in one volume of the British Library's collection ADD MSS 20216.

to send to London, for publication in the pro-Napoleon *Morning Chronicle*, a copy of the 'Remonstrance' (see pp. 53–4) of August 1816. Meanwhile, the doctor's busy pen was fully deployed. Apart from his letters to Finlaison, he transmitted to Plantation House a whole series of complaints and requests on the part of the French, including a proposal by Bonaparte that, in order to overcome the 'Emperor-General' impasse, he should go under the name of Baron Duroc (a former Grand Marshal, killed in battle). There was no sequel to this potentially interesting idea, although Lowe did respond with the thought that instead of calling the captive General Bonaparte, he should address him as Napoleon Bonaparte – which he proceeded to do, though this gave no satisfaction whatever to Bonaparte.

Among other communications from O'Meara to the Governor was one (31 October 1816) describing a long conversation with Bonaparte – or rather a monologue from him – about the Battle of Waterloo. Another such historical reminiscence was the subject of a memorandum from O'Meara (28 January 1817) recording Bonaparte's plans for invading England, which he would have proclaimed a republic. Obviously the prisoner, frustrated by the atmosphere of backbiting and rivalries between the members of his own staff, found in the personable young Irishman a ready and sympathetic audience.

O'Meara also played a part in the Affair of the Bust. This marked one of several occasions when Lowe was blamed for something of which he was innocent. It began with the arrival from London at St Helena of a British naval storeship, in which had been shipped a bust of the King of Rome, Bonaparte's son. Who commissioned it is not clear – obviously one of Bonaparte's sympathisers in England. The London agents who shipped it entrusted it to a non-British sailor, variously described as Rethwick or Radovitch. Captain Lamb, commanding the ship, knew nothing of the bust until arrival at St Helena. Plantation House was informed of the matter, and Lowe's first instinct was to withhold it, at least until he could seek Bathurst's opinion, on the grounds that its dispatch constituted impermissible communication with the outer world. Reference to London would have meant a delay of several months, and Sir Thomas Reade sensibly argued that as a piece of marble could not possibly contain anything illicit it should be sent to Longwood at once.

This was done, and Bonaparte received it with understandable delight. But he also told O'Meara[19] that he knew when the bust had first arrived in the storeship and knew further that orders had been given for it to be broken up. 'I intended,' he told O'Meara, 'if it had not been given to have made such a complaint as would have caused every Englishman's hair to stand on end with horror. I would have told a tale which would have made the mothers of England execrate him [Lowe] as a monster in human shape.' O'Meara says he tried to convince Bonaparte of his error, but in vain. He insisted on believing, or pretending to believe, that orders had been given for the destruction of the bust, blackguarding Lowe for having given such orders.

These battles, so futile in themselves yet so characteristic of the poisonous relationship between Longwood and Plantation House, continued unabated. While there is abundant proof of Bonaparte's ill will and bad temper, Lowe for his part cannot be freed from charges of prejudice and insensitivity. In October 1817, for example, O'Meara reported to the Governor that in his, O'Meara's, opinion Bonaparte was suffering from hepatitis. Lowe refused to accept the report, accused O'Meara of being in collusion with the French, and forbade the use of the alarming word.[20] Sometime before this, Lowe showed, quite unnecessarily, his pettiness when he wrote to Bertrand explaining that he, Lowe, would have been quite within his rights in withholding a fine set of Chinese chessmen, sent as a present to Bonaparte by the Hon. John Elphinstone, then head of the East India Company's establishment in China. Elphinstone's brother's life had been saved by Napoleon's personal intervention just before the Battle of Waterloo (see p. 31). And now this gesture was a graceful and generous expression of gratitude towards a defeated enemy. The only trouble was that the pieces were marked with eagles and the letter N. Despite the rules, Lowe let them through, and then spoiled the effect by his note to Bertrand. There was a furious reaction from Longwood. Bertrand, as usual transmitting Bonaparte's own words, replied that 'the Emperor will not accept of favours from anybody, nor be indebted for anything to the caprice of anyone . . .'

But in contrast to such heavy-handed tactlessness on the Governor's part, when it came to moaning and groaning, the French party exceeded all reasonable limits. As Lowe wrote despairingly to Bathurst in September 1817, 'complaint being the object, everything which can give food to it is most greedily sought after, and everything which tends to remove it as ungraciously received'. The Longwood ethos sometimes went further than a stream of complaint. A long and angry letter from Bertrand to Lowe, of 30 September 1817, only a few weeks after the Affair of the Bust and the present of the chess-men, repeats all the earlier objections to the restrictions imposed on Bonaparte's movements, and then goes on:[21] 'the question can be put in two words – "do you or do you not wish to kill the Emperor? If you persist in your course of action, you will yourself have answered in the affirmative, and unhappily the objective will probably be achieved after a few months of agony".' (In fact, Bonaparte lived for another three and a half years and then succumbed to an illness which had little con-nection with his refusal to take exercise while the hateful restrictions were in force).

The harassed Governor, beset by French-inspired rumours that he had been censured for his conduct by the government in London, had the satisfaction in October 1816 of knowing that his political masters, far from disapproving, applauded his stance. 'I am commanded to convey to you,' Bathurst wrote, 'His Royal Highness' entire approbation of your conduct under the difficult circumstances in which you have been recently placed, in consequence of the intemperance of General Bonaparte, the general insubordination of his attendants, and the insolence of General Bertrand . . .' Years later, on Lowe's arrival back in England after Bonaparte's death, Bathurst recorded in a dispatch the King's (the former Regent was now on the throne) 'general approbation' of Lowe's governorship. 'Placed as you have been in a situation which must, under any circumstances, have been one of heavy responsibility . . . you discharged your arduous trust with strict fidelity, discretion and humanity.' When Lowe, in November 1821, had an audience of the King, the latter refused a formal hand-kiss and instead grasped Lowe's hand and shook it heartily. 'I congratulate you most sincerely upon your return, after a trial the most arduous and exemplary that perhaps any man ever had.'[22] These were the views of a sovereign who had abandoned the Whiggism of his youth, when Charles James Fox and Sheridan had been his cronies, and had became as ardent a supporter of the war with France as his father had been. Holland and his Whig friends were very far from sharing such opinions. But whatever may be thought of Lowe's record at St Helena, it seems tragically unjust that the praise accorded in 1821 had no sequel and that he died an unhappy and unhonoured man.*

A series of Englishmen who might be said to have had, or who had tried to have, daily contact with Bonaparte were the army orderly officers. They were required to verify the prisoner's presence at least twice in twenty-four hours, to report on any untoward activities at Longwood, and to ensure that the 'General' and his attendants were indoors by 9 p.m. The purpose of all these regulations was to guard against and give warning of any attempt at escape. But given Bonaparte's determination not to be seen by his English guardians, the unfortunate officer on duty could find himself in a difficult situation.

---

* See Appendix 1.

The earliest of them was Captain Poppleton, of the 53rd Regiment, which assumed garrison duties at St Helena in November 1815. He seems to have avoided major difficulties, although he rarely succeeded in carrying out to the letter his instructions to witness the captive's presence twice daily. Far from resenting him, Bonaparte appears to have taken rather a liking to him, and on one occasion (31 August 1816) sent for him and told him to tell the officers of his regiment – of which Poppleton was senior captain – that he, Bonaparte, looked on them as 'brave men and good soldiers', whom he would always 'be happy to see'. Reporting the conversation, Poppleton said that Bonaparte 'was in very good humour and we parted with a great deal of civility on his part'. The captain was almost certainly a crypto-Bonapartist because on relinquishing his post he accepted the present of a snuffbox[‡‡] from the Emperor, which he must have known was against the rules. On returning to England, he did the correct thing by informing Bathurst of the present, but that did not save him from Lowe's censure, once he got to hear of the matter, for having, as he saw it, betrayed trust.

[‡‡]The snuffbox remained in the possession of Poppleton's family, who lived in County Galway. His granddaughter, Mrs Caldwell, tells the story (*Old Irish Life*, 1912, p. 226) of how an inquisitive visitor, sometime in the 1850s, found at the bottom of the box a folded paper, which had been lying there undiscovered for nearly forty years. It was a letter from Bonaparte himself to Las Cases in Europe, sending messages to Bonapartists in France, and giving instructions as to how the King of Rome should be brought up. Las Cases was by now dead, but the missive was forwarded to his son. The incident shows that Bonaparte was ready – who can blame him? – to take every opportunity to evade Lowe's vigilance. It also shows how partially ineffective Lowe's rules and regulations were; letters to and from abroad passed into and out of Longwood with the regularity of an organised postal service.

Poppleton was succeeded by Captain Blakeney, of the 66th Regiment which took over from the 53rd. He held the post for a year. He did not seem to have experienced any particular difficulties, but this was certainly not the case with the officer who took over from him. This was the inspector of the St Helena militia force called Lyster, who bore the local rank of lieutenant-colonel. Bonaparte convinced himself, mistakenly, that Lyster had served in Lowe's Corsican Rangers, which meant that he was totally unacceptable. He said as much in a letter written by Bertrand. The letter was insulting to Lowe, with its accusation of Lyster having been Lowe's 'creature for many years . . . having no other will, no other conscience than yours, that is to say of an avowed enemy'. The Governor, whose proneness to gaffes was such a feature of his behaviour, showed the letter to Lyster who, considering his honour as an officer impugned, challenged Bertrand to a duel. When there was no response, he threatened, in a follow-up communication, to horsewhip the Grand Marshal. He had quickly to be ordered away from Longwood and Lowe had to apologise to Bertrand.[23]

Captain Nicholls, also of the 66th Regiment, was next to be appointed. He had an undeniably hard time, and his reports strike a tragi-comic note. In that dated 15 May 1819[24] he complains that 'in the execution of my duty yesterday, I was upon my feet upwards of *ten hours* endeavouring to procure a sight of Napoleon Bonaparte, either in his little garden or at one of his windows . . . during the whole of this time I was exposed to the observations and remarks of not only the French servants, but also to the gardeners and other persons employed about Longwood House'. Poor Nicholls continued to meet the same difficulties. One day in July 1819, Montholon told him that Napoleon usually walked about in the billiard room after dinner, where he might be seen, if not through the window, then through the keyhole. Nicholls refused to resort to such antics and a few days later was again complaining that he had been ten hours walking about in the garden in bad weather, without seeing 'the General'. He had no better luck in trying to deliver a letter from the Governor addressed to 'Napoleon Bonaparte'. In vain he tried to get Montholon, Bertrand and the valet Marchand to receive it. Finally Nicholls's superiors instructed him to enter Longwood through the back door, go towards Bonaparte's dressingroom, knocking at every closed door, and, if he found the door barred or locked, to leave the letter on a table.

Nicholls also had more general, if not very helpful, instructions about how to make his way into Bonaparte's presence. Nobody on the British side, and certainly not Nicholls, wanted to use force to achieve the objective (Bonaparte had declared that he would shoot anyone trying to effect an entry without his consent). So the ludicrous result was that Nicholls had to peep through an open window at the Corsican ogre in his bath: 'he had a most ghastly appearance', he reported.

When Bonaparte took to gardening, which he did towards the end of his captivity with an energy and enthusiasm typical of most of his chosen activities, it became much easier, indeed simple, for Nicholls to bear witness to his continued existence. But despite this improvement, he had had enough, and on 9 February 1820 he was at his own request succeeded at his post by Captain Lutyens. He, too, had no problem in observing the General working in the garden or shooting marauding chickens and goats because they had dared to interfere with his horticultural experiments.

By the end of 1820, Lutyens's reports, in the context of the captive's increasing debilities, had come to read almost like a medical journal. Unlike Poppleton, he does not seem to have had any converse with the General, although he does report, in mid-February 1821 (less than three months before Bonaparte's death), a chance meeting with him near the stables: 'I took off my hat, which the General returned by raising his hat on his head . . . he looked very pale and languid.' Lutyens was replaced as orderly officer in mid-April after falling out with Lowe. Bonaparte wanted to present the 20th Regiment (later the Lancashire Fusiliers), which had assumed garrison duties on the island, with the three volumes, sent earlier to him by an English admirer, of Cox's *Life of Marlborough*. The books, which were left without explanation in Lutyens's room, contained the proscribed Imperial title, and when Lowe heard of the present he caused the commanding officer of the 20th to write to Lutyens suggesting he should return the books to Montholon. Lutyens reluctantly complied, writing a disrespectful letter to his colonel and showing signs of insubordination towards the Governor. As a result, he was relieved of his post. As he left Longwood, possibly by now a closet Bonapartist, Montholon made him a little speech, in which he said he had been asked by Bonaparte to express his, Bonaparte's, satisfaction with Lutyens's tour of duty, together with the hope that, health permitting, 'he shall have the pleasure of seeing you'.

The episode of the *Marlborough* books does not leave a good taste in the mouth. Bonaparte's wish to honour a British regiment showed a professional respect for the military vocation that Lowe should have recognised, instead of insisting on the letter of the law. Bonaparte's admiration for the 'brave men and good soldiers' of the British army is comparable with his even greater feeling, fostered in *Bellerophon* and *Northumberland*, for the Royal Navy. His refusal to be accompanied by a British officer if walking or riding beyond the official limits, and his childish cat-and-mouse game with the orderly officers, does not seem to have been inspired by any personal dislike or antipathy, but principally by his resolve not to accept the status of a prisoner subject to the hated Lowe's authority. That hatred was, of course, intensely personal, directed against Lowe as a man rather than as a soldier – a status which Bonaparte, in his paranoiac moods, liked to deny.

What the soldiers and sailors thought of Bonaparte is not easy to divine. Some of them, such as Poppleton, finished up by being anti-Lowe, implying a degree of sympathy with Bonaparte. Others testified in Lowe's favour in the latter's 1823 case against O'Meara; they included Nicholls, despite his differences with the Governor. Among this last group was also Sir George Bingham, who was second-in-command of troops at St Helena from 1815 to 1819, and at one time colonel of the 53rd. He began by adopting a friendly attitude towards Bonaparte, visiting him and inviting him to lunch in the officers' mess. He was courteously received at Longwood, but the invitation was declined. Later, Bingham was invited to dine at Longwood. This was during the first few months of the captivity when ten Englishmen and three wives, all of them of naval or military status, got their feet under the Imperial dinner table.

It was not, according to Bingham, an enjoyable occasion:

> it was a most superb dinner which lasted only forty minutes, at the end of which we retired into the drawing room to play cards. The dessert service was Sèvres china, with gold knives, forks and spoons. The coffee cups were the most beautiful I have ever seen . . . the dinner was stupid enough; the people who lived with him scarcely spoke out of a whisper; and he was so much engaged in eating that he hardly said a word to anyone. He had so filled the room with wax candles that it was as hot as an oven'.[25]

Later on, in January 1817, by which time the relations between Longwood and Plantation House were at their lowest ebb, the Governor sent Bingham to see Bonaparte with the idea of effecting reconciliation. But he was coldly received, and the same *froideur* was displayed two months later when Bingham and his wife had half an hour's conversation with 'the General'. In 1819 the Binghams returned to England, much to Lowe's regret.

One insight into the attitude of the British military towards Bonaparte is afforded by the account of his meeting with the officers of the first battalion of the 66th Regiment. They went to Longwood, ranged themselves around the walls of the salon, and awaited 'the Emperor's' appearance. The result was disappointing, according to the testimony of Walter Henry, the regimental doctor. 'His general look,' he wrote, 'was more that of an obese Spanish or Portuguese friar, than the hero of modern times.'[26] Bonaparte walked round the room, speaking to most of the officers, his remarks being more or less interpreted by Bingham and Bertrand, neither of them fluent in the other's language. As the officers walked back to their cantonment, the general feeling, according to Henry, was one of disillusion: 'a fascinating prestige, which we had cherished all our lives, then vanished like gossamer in the sun . . . at our mess dinner the same evening, our illustrious neighbour had evidently fallen off by one-half, from our notions concerning him of the day before.'

Against this rather unflattering picture must be placed another and different impression. In June 1817 Lord Amherst, British Ambassador to China, stopped at St Helena on his homeward journey. It was Lowe's intention to see whether the Ambassador could serve as a mediator. Bonaparte, on his side, planned to use the distinguished visitor to relay his grievances direct to the Prince Regent, without going through Lowe. In the event, Amherst listened to the prisoner's complaints, undertook to report them to the Prince Regent, but gave it as his own opinion that they were unfounded. The members of the Ambassador's mission were all introduced to Bonaparte, and one of them, Mr Ellis, left a long account of the conversation (given in Appendix XI of Scott's *Life of Napoleon Bonaparte*) in which he writes of Bonaparte's 'great and unjustifiable bitterness respecting Sir Hudson Lowe . . . it is difficult to conceive any complaints more unreasonable'. Despite this judgement, Ellis found Bonaparte's general bearing and manner dignified, affable and pleasing: 'had [he] been in plenitude of his powers, his manner could not have been more dignified or more calculated to command respect.' The medical member of the Ambassador's staff was rather more detached: 'whatever may be his [Bonaparte's] general habit, he can behave himself very prettily if he pleases.' The contrast between the disappointment of the officers of the 66th and Ellis's admiration can only be explained by the trouble Bonaparte took to show himself in the best possible light to a visitor on whose cooperation he was counting.§§

Another English visitor to Longwood, of whom much was hoped by the French group, was Mr Ricketts, a cousin of Lord Liverpool. His journey home from the East, like that of so many other travellers, brought him to St Helena in the spring of 1819. Almost the last of Bonaparte's 'outside' visitors, he had four hours' conversation with him on 2 April. In his account, he did not think that his interlocutor showed 'any particular marks indicative of his being afflicted with the liver or any other severe bodily complaint'.[27] Ricketts found 'his manners were rough and brusque, consequently to me far from fascinating'. Before Ricketts arrived, Bonaparte had drawn up a list of complaints and requests, including a wish to be moved from the island 'because I am suffering from chronic hepatitis'; a desire that whatever happened he might be 'near a man of honour who understands the forms of politeness' (an obvious dig at Lowe); the return of O'Meara or another French or English doctor with 'no military tie'; and authorisation by Liverpool of direct correspondence – i.e. not via Lowe – between himself and the Prime Minister, 'or with a peer of the realm such as Lord Holland'.

§§In his remarks to Ellis, Napoleon spoke of England's [Britain's] relationship to continental Europe in words which, essentially, were re-echoed by General de Gaulle nearly 150 years later, when he vetoed Britain's entry into the European Community: 'England should look wholly to commerce and naval affairs; she can never be a Continental power and in the attempt [to be one] must be ruined.'

Whatever it was Ricketts said on his return to London, it must have been very far from what Bonaparte was hoping, for in the following July Bathurst wrote to Lowe that 'nothing could have been more fortunate than Mr Ricketts' visit to St Helena . . . he has given the most satisfactory reports concerning the real state of the business, and saw through all the manoeuvres which were practised to impose on him'.

Admiral Sir Pulteney Malcolm, whom we have already met being introduced to Bonaparte soon after his arrival (see p. 82) established a remarkably favourable rapport with 'the General'. Lady Malcolm to whom Bonaparte was equally agreeable, left a diary record of her encounters which, though recording her own impressions and memories, also include accounts of what passed between Bonaparte and her husband, the result of what Malcolm afterwards told his wife. The indelible message of the diary as a whole is that Bonaparte made a point of being affable to the Malcolms, who in turn, according to a nearly invariable rule of human behaviour, were friendly to him. The contrast with the relationships with Lowe could not have been greater. The Governor was surely correct when he wrote, after his bruising last meeting with his prisoner, that the latter's purpose was to 'lower me in the Admiral's opinion and to make an invidious distinction between us'.

Not long after his arrival on the island, Malcolm was closeted with Bonaparte for two hours, during which 'the General' spoke of Trafalgar, plans for the invasion of England, Waterloo, the Bourbons ('they will never tranquillise France') and when the British should have made peace. Several times during the conversation, Bonaparte laughed so heartily that Las Cases, in the adjoining room, said to Malcolm's officers who were waiting to be presented that 'the Emperor was very much pleased when he laughed so heartily'. Three weeks later, Sir Pulteney had a four-hour session, when Bonaparte developed his familiar complaints against Lowe: 'He has not the character of an Englishman, he is a Prussian soldier'. Malcolm, awkwardly placed, tried to persuade Bonaparte that despite the Governor's manner, he was well intentioned, but this only caused the other to say, with surprising honesty, that it was just that manner that irritated him: 'he cannot please me, call it *enfantillage* [childishness] or what you will, so it is.'

It was not so much *enfantillage* as the desire to cause trouble and make propaganda that lay behind the affair of Bonaparte's silver plate. In September 1816 he ordered that this should be sold locally, the ostensible reason being that the proceeds were needed to pay for food and provisions. That at least is how the message reached the outer world, where it had considerable effect (see the reference in Byron's poem 'The Age of Bronze', p. 124).

But at the time, O'Meara told Sir Thomas Reade (23 September 1816) that 'the object of selling the plate is very evident and does not require me to point it out to you'. To his friend Finlaison in London, he wrote of the large quantities of food eaten daily by the French party, whom he described as 'except one or two [these would have included Bonaparte himself, who ate and drank sparingly and spent little time at table##] the greatest gluttons and epicures I ever saw', consuming every day 'three or four times as much as any English family composed of a similar number of persons'. This is supported by what Montholon told Gorrequer, the Governor's private secretary, in March 1818. Far too much wine, he commented, was being supplied to Longwood, as well as too much bread and meat: 'we have no reproaches against the Governor, we do not complain of anything and we have abundance of all that is needed'.

##Napoleon used to joke about eating quickly. As First Consul he once said to his dinner guests: 'if you want to eat well, you eat with the Second Consul, if you want to eat badly, with the Third Consul, but if you want to eat quickly, you eat with me.'

This seems to dispose of the idea that the Longwood party, through lack of means, was living on short rations. There can be little doubt that the sale of the silver was a deliberate attempt to show Lowe and the British government in a bad light. Bonaparte's words, in December 1818, are as self-revealing as it is possible to be: 'whatever they say, I can make or unmake the reputation of the Governor . . . all I choose to say of him, of his bad behaviour, of his ideas of poisoning me, will be believed.'[28]

Lowe, for understandable reasons, did not like the idea of the tête-à-tête meetings between Bonaparte and the Admiral, from which he was excluded. Although Malcolm loyally reported to the Governor anything of importance that passed, it was virtually inevitable that a prickly man like Lowe should think – understandably so – that Bonaparte, by showing consistent friendliness to the Malcolms, was seeking to emphasise his rejection of the Governor and his system. Like some other people, Malcolm found Lowe difficult to deal with, so by the time the Admiral left for England at the end of his appointment, relations between the two men were greatly strained, though not entirely because of differences over the treatment of Bonaparte.[29]

The Malcolms, until they finally took their leave in July 1817, had several more meetings with Bonaparte, sometimes as a couple, sometimes the Admiral going alone. The talk ranged over a wide field, much of it involving Napoleonic campaigns and reminiscences, as well as the political situation in France. When Lady Malcolm was present, he was especially gallant, on one occasion challenging her to a session of chess, in which they both won a game. On the whole, Bonaparte steered clear of his favoured pastime of complaining about Lowe. But every so often, when he was alone with the Admiral, he reverted to form.

Malcolm sensibly observed that most of the misunderstandings were the result of misrepresentations, misconceptions and the want of direct conversation between the Governor and his charge. Bonaparte, with engaging frankness, admitted as much: 'the Governor does not understand my character, he has never seen me but when I was irritated, and then I spoke folly.' The Admiral, whatever disputes may have arisen between him and Lowe, seems always to have done his best to defend him and to reassure Bonaparte that he, Lowe, was only concerned to make him as comfortable as possible. 'Bah' was the only response. But Bonaparte's relations with the Malcolms remained agreeable to the end. At their final meeting, he thanked them for coming to see him and Mesdames Bertrand and Montholon, 'in their misfortune', and gave Lady Malcolm a fine Sèvres coffee cup and saucer. On bidding farewell, Malcolm introduced his successor, Admiral Plampin, to whom Bonaparte, curious as ever, addressed questions about the displacement of ships.

Meanwhile, the Lowe–O'Meara relationship continued to deteriorate. In November 1817 there was a flaming row, when the doctor declined to report on his conversations with his patient. Lowe upbraided him, but O'Meara said he refused to become a spy or *mouton*. The doctor, who had several times tried to resign his post, was at last, in July 1818, ordered, on instructions from London, to quit Longwood. He was put on board a London-bound ship. At his leave-taking interview with Bonaparte, the latter embraced him, gave him two snuffboxes and a statuette, and said, '*Adieu, O'Meara, nous ne nous reverrons jamais, soyez heureux*'.

It is difficult to establish the rights and wrongs of the O'Meara affair, all the more so because his record of events is so often in direct contradiction with Lowe's. One side of the case is to argue that he was a conscientious doctor, performing his professional duty. He certainly reported to Lowe in October 1817 the possibility that Bonaparte might be suffering from chronic hepatitis. This was potentially alarming, but was it a correct diagnosis or part of a Bonaparte-inspired ploy to persuade the government in London to ease the restrictions or even to move the captive from St Helena altogether?* Some accounts say that Bonaparte bought, with a large bribe, O'Meara's cooperation in testifying that his condition was worse than it really was.[30] On O'Meara's departure, his former patient gave him a letter asking Jérome Bonaparte or Eugène de Beauharnais (the Emperor's stepson) to pay him £4,000,[31] and also made arrangements for him to have a pension of £320 a year.

The problem about the true state of Bonaparte's health is further complicated by the conduct of General Gourgaud, who left St Helena in March 1818. When he got to London, he told Henry Goulburn, Under-Secretary for War, that reports about Bonaparte's failing health were unfounded, that he could escape whenever he chose, and that O'Meara had been duped by his patient. But only a few months later, Gourgaud made a complete recantation, and wrote to Napoleon's wife, Marie-Louise, as well as to the Russian emperor that Bonaparte was dying and that Lowe was killing him by pinpricks.

What does emerge with startling clarity from the O'Meara affairs is that from the moment he left St Helena the Irishman made it his life's mission to get his own back on Hudson Lowe. Even during the voyage home, when his ship touched at Ascension, he told various naval officers whom he met there that Lowe had tried to persuade him to kill the prisoner.[32] Arrived in England, he repeated the insinuations in a letter to the Admiralty, with the result that he was dismissed from the navy. Only temporarily daunted, he produced, early in 1819, a pamphlet attacking Lowe, and went on, after Bonaparte's death, to publish, in 1822, his *Voice from St Helena*, consisting

*Bonaparte's own account of his meeting with Lord Amherst provides a striking example of his readiness to resort, when it suited him, to play-acting: 'I shammed sick to receive Lord Amherst . . . I won his Lordship, whom I knew to be a not very intelligent person' (Johnston, op. cit., p. 495).

in part of a sustained and powerful denunciation of Lowe. Coming from the doctor who, alone of the British, had been close to and tended Bonaparte for nearly three years, the book had a great success, brought temporary fame to O'Meara and ruined Lowe's already tarnished reputation.[33] Byron gave two lines to the vengeful doctor in his 1823 poem. 'The Age of Bronze':

'And the stiff surgeon who maintained his cause,
Hath lost his place and gained the world's applause.'

However necessary and approved internationally, Bonaparte's captivity at St Helena is a sad and sorry story. The former Emperor's unhappiness, frustration, the constant sense of grievance, the frequent squabbling among the members of his little court, his worsening health – all these are elements in a saga of almost unrelieved gloom. The episode of an impromptu picnic[34] in British company shines forth, therefore, like an unexpected shaft of sunlight. The British family concerned was that of Sir William Doveton, a member for many years of the St Helena's Governor's Council, who had been knighted for his services. His house, Mount Pleasant, was about five miles from Longwood, and there, on the morning of 4 October 1820, while taking an after-breakfast stroll, he saw a party of horsemen approaching.

They proved to be from Longwood. Montholon dismounted and told Doveton that 'the Emperor' would like to come into the house and rest a while. Doveton bade him welcome. Bonaparte walked in and sat on a sofa, and there was a rather stilted conversation, Bertrand acting as a far from adequate interpreter. The granddaughters of the house, whose noses Bonaparte, always playful with children, gently pinched, afforded light relief; he also rewarded them with pieces of liquorice, which he produced from a small tortoiseshell box. Sir William hospitably offered refreshment, which Bonaparte declined, explaining that they had brought their own breakfast.

A table was set up on the lawn; Sir William was invited to join the party and did in fact supply some of the food. Justice was done to 'a cold pie, potted meat, cold turkey, curried fowl, coffee, dates, almonds, oranges and a very fine salad'. Bonaparte placed Sir William on his right, drank champagne with him, and later asked if his daughter, the mother of the children, could join them.

The meal finished, the whole party went back into the house, where Bonaparte questioned the Dovetons about their drinking habits (he seemed to think that English people were habitual over-consumers of alcohol – 'drink' and 'drunk' were two English words which he used a lot in conversation). Doveton, recording the event, wrote that 'General Bonaparte was in good health, his face is astonishingly fat, and his body and thighs very round and plump'. Perhaps he was not a good observer, or Bonaparte was having a good day. In fact, from now on his health deteriorated fast, and by the end of the year he was seriously unwell and unable to keep food down. Only a few months of his miserable life were left.

4

Death and Burial

On 5 July 1821 an anonymous note was delivered to Lady
Holland who, with her husband, was in Paris. It read:
'*Bonaparte est mort le 5 Mai d'un abcès à l'estomac.*'[1] This was
followed the next day by a respectful letter from Hudson Lowe,
who wrote of the 'compassionate interest which your ladyship
has so constantly and in so generous a manner shown towards
the remarkable person who had been so long under my charge'.
It was, Lowe explained, 'beyond the powers of medicine to
have saved him, though every assistance was afforded him'. Ten
days later came another letter from Lowe, informing Lady
Holland that Bonaparte had bequeathed her a snuffbox, originally given to him by Pope Pius VI. On going through the
deceased's personal effects at Longwood, Lowe had opened the
snuffbox and discovered it had a card in the ex-Emperor's hand-
writing: '*L'Empereur Napoléon à Lady Holland, témoignage de
satisfaction et d'estime.*'[2] Some months later, the box was delivered to Holland House by Counts Bertrand and Montholon,
liberated from their island fortress by their master's death. They
were wearing full Imperial uniform, which caused the implac-
ably anti-monarchist Holland to wonder how such people, after
devoting themselves to 'a man of great intellect', could imagine
they honoured his memory 'by aping the absurd forms of other
sovereigns or pretenders'.[3]

Lowe's first letter to Lady Holland, with its reference to 'a remarkable person', suggests that, faced with the solemnity of death, he was affected by feelings of remorse. Many would think that this was no more than appropriate. Up to a very late stage, Lowe – and Bathurst in London – had been sceptical or openly incredulous of reports that Bonaparte was seriously ill. With O'Meara's departure in July 1818, the prisoner was left (due to his own obstinacy) without a doctor. Lowe did make efforts to supply one. O'Meara's warnings that his patient might die without medical aid evidently had some influence with the mistrustful Governor, for in that same July he agreed to the appointment as medical officer at Longwood of another Irishman, James Verling, surgeon to an artillery regiment.

He spoke good French, and Bonaparte had met him on board *Northumberland*. He might have been very suitable, but Bonaparte refused to have anything to do with him, so that the only patients Verling acquired during his fourteen months' stay at Longwood were its other French residents. In January 1819, however, Bonaparte had an alarming seizure and medical assistance became essential. Bertrand was permitted, given the captive's continued refusal to see Verling, to call in Dr John Stokoe, another naval doctor. He had arrived in the island in June 1817 as the surgeon aboard the flagship of the incoming Admiral, Plampin. As a friend of O'Meara's, he had visited the latter at Longwood, when he had been presented to Bonaparte, who seemed to have liked him. So much so that when Lowe initially proposed to replace O'Meara with another doctor, Bonaparte himself suggested Stokoe.

The latter, aware of the trouble into which O'Meara had got himself, begged to be excused, and Verling got the post, but not the full duties, of doctor at Longwood. The urgent summons of January 1819 had, for obvious professional reasons, to be answered by Stokoe, whatever his misgivings. Over a period of four days, he examined Bonaparte and diagnosed a chronic infection of the liver. Reporting to Lowe, he added that, to make this diagnosis, he had questioned Bonaparte and others of the Longwood group about previous development of the illness – a course of action necessary for any doctor coming new to a case – and had also discussed possible terms of employment at Longwood.[4] Both Lowe and the Admiral chose to suspect Stokoe of conniving with the French, just as Lowe had had the same suspicions, though with rather more reasons, about O'Meara.

Stokoe, at his own request, left Longwood and returned to England, momentarily thankful to have avoided the perilous morass represented by such a medical appointment. Any hopes he had were soon dashed, however, by the decision of the Admiralty to send him straight back to St Helena to undergo a naval court-martial on charges of having breached regulations about dealing with the French group. The result of the case was the dismissal of Stokoe from the navy. It was a harsh and un-deserved sentence. His case was taken up by the pro-Bonopartist *Morning Chronicle* in April 1819 and he was sub-sequently awarded a small pension from the Civil List.

These events meant that Bonaparte, who maintained his veto against Verling, was again left without a doctor. By the time the thoroughly unsuitable Corsican Doctor Antommacchi (chosen in Rome by Bonaparte's mother and her half-brother, Cardinal Fesch) arrived in the island in September 1819, the prisoner/patient had been without a personal physician for eighteen months and had seen no doctor of any kind for eight months. This was because of his refusal to accept any doctor nominated by Lowe, but it meant that it was not until April 1821, within a few weeks of his death, that he finally consented to the attend-ance of a British doctor, this time without prior conditions. This was Doctor Arnott, the principal medical officer on the island, who had already, eighteen months earlier, offered his services and then withdrawn the offer when faced with the conditions laid down by Bonaparte. Having for so long spurned the services of a British doctor, there is no knowing why Bonaparte consented to Arnott. The only reason he gave was in the words 'I don't know if he is a good doctor, but he had a good appearance, I will receive him'.[5] Arnott first saw his patient on 1 April and daily, sometimes twice daily, thereafter. He was only three years younger than Bonaparte, who got on well with him, bequeathing him the customary snuffbox, on which he had scratched the letter N. A sample of their dialogue together, consisting largely of a fusillade of questions, evidence of Bonaparte's insatiable curiosity on every subject, is given in Bertrand's memoirs.[6] A temporary improvement in his condition in the second week of April gave him increased confidence in Arnott, whose manners, ability to speak Italian and general disposition made him an agreeable person for the dying man to talk to.

Arnott was adamant until almost the very last in denying that his patient was seriously ill. Whether this was because he had been influenced by Lowe's and Bathurst's contention that Bonaparte was all along malingering, in order to strengthen the case for a more relaxed regime, or whether he, Arnott, genuinely and as a doctor could not discern the grave symptoms of his patient can only be guessed at. Some French historians are critical of him for his persistence in error. It is indeed difficult to acquit him of such charges. Antommacchi, whom Bonaparte could not abide, had already come to the conclusion (like O'Meara) that the patient was suffering from hepatitis and could not last long unless removed from the island. But it was not until 27 April, despite the fact that Bonaparte was wracked with fever and vomited frequently, that Arnott told the Governor that the situation was serious. A few days later, on 3 May, the Governor came to Longwood and offered the services of the chief medical officer and of the head naval surgeon. He admitted that, despite rumours to the contrary, he himself had not believed that the ex-Emperor was seriously ill. He now knew that it was so.[7] On 5 May, just after sunset, Bonaparte expired, his death witnessed by most of the French contingent. Arnott, standing with Antommacchi at the head of the bed, was the only Englishman present, apart from Captain Crockat the orderly officer who had succeeded Lutyens. Bonaparte was four months short of his fifty-second birthday.

It is not the purpose of this book to go into the disputed question of the causes of death. Stomach cancer, hepatitis, gastric ulcers and psychological disarray are all among the possibilities, to say nothing of poison theories. One of these postulates that Montholon, aggrieved by the attentions paid by Bonaparte to his wife, was the murderer.

A book written jointly by a French historian, René Maury, and a descendant of Montholon, François de Candé-Montholon, was published in Paris in 2000[†] based on recently discovered letters exchanged between Montholon and his wife. It suggests that a *ménage à trois* prevailed at Longwood, in which Napoleon and Montholon shared the bed of the latter's wife, who had a history of being free with her favours. The daughter, Josephine, born to Mme Montholon at St Helena in 1819, was almost certainly Napoleon's.

The authors claim that once Mme Montholon had returned with her children to France in 1819, Montholon conceived and carried out the idea of administering small doses of arsenic to Bonaparte with the aim of making him sufficiently ill for the British government to remove him from St Helena, thus enabling Montholon to rejoin his wife in France.

The unforeseen and unintended result was that the arsenic reacted violently with the calomel and other emetics that the doctors were administering to the patient, and this led to his death. If this story is true, it disposes not only of the argument that Bonaparte died of stomach cancer but also of the claim that 'the British' (presumably Hudson Lowe, acting with or without instructions from London) arranged for him to be poisoned. There has never been any real evidence to support this theory,

[†] *Napoléon, l'énigme résolue*, Albin Michel.

but that has not, of course, prevented it from being frequently repeated, above all by French Napoleonists and/or Anglophobes.

The Maury-Montholon story is certainly consonant with the findings of scientists in Paris, reported in June 2001, that what were thought to be samples of Napoleon's hair contained 'high levels of arsenic.' In fact there was nothing new here. Earlier tests, by Swedish and Scottish dentists and doctors (notably Dr Forshufvud of Göteborg) had found arsenic to be present in the hair.

The most generally accepted, though still disputed, cause of death was cancer of the stomach. Bonaparte himself believed, on the basis that his father had died from cancer, that this was what he was suffering from. '*Oh mon pylore, mon pylore*'‡ he would exclaim, holding his side, when afflicted with severe abdominal pains. The whole drama of his death is shot through with rumour, myth and legend, some of the material so far-fetched as to be farcical. Stories of his escape abound. One had him getting to Brazil, from there to England by the spring of 1819; another contends that he never went to St Helena, his apparent presence at Longwood being accounted for by the appearance of a double, a certain Rifleman Rombeaud or Robeaud, substituted by Fouché.

Possibly the most far-fetched of all these tales is that woven by a French writer, Rétif de la Bretonne, whose book *Anglais, Rendez-nous Napoléon* (1969) claims that at the burial under the willow trees in the vale of Geranium, the body of one of the senior servants at Longwood, who had died in 1818, was substituted for that of the ex-Emperor; the latter's remains were then spirited away, to finish up in ... Westminster Abbey. Would Napoleon have been pleased or not by this supreme mark of respect from his British enemy? What is certain is that once

‡The pylorus is the opening from the stomach into the duo-denum.

death had intervened, Lowe, the Sicilian bandit, the staff clerk, the executioner, the spy, the Prussian soldier and all the other disagreeable personae ascribed by the prisoner to his hated guardian, behaved with dignity and decorum.

Early on the morning of 6 May, he came to Longwood, accompanied by the Admiral and other officers, and paid his respects. It was the first time he had seen his prisoner for nearly five years. Among those accompanying the Governor was Captain Marryat, RN, the future author of *Mr Midshipman Easy* and other novels, who made a drawing of the dead man lying on his simple iron bedstead. Lowe's feelings at the time are best described in his own words, uttered to two officers at Plantation House when he first received the news of Bonaparte's death: 'Well, gentlemen, he was England's greatest enemy and mine too, but I forgive him everything. On the death of a great man like him, we should only feel deep concern and regret.'

Later that day, an autopsy was performed by Antommacchi in the presence of five English doctors – despite the fact that Bonaparte had specified that Arnott was to be the only English doctor to see his lifeless body. The findings were obviously going to be important for Lowe and, indirectly, for Lord Liverpool's government. If it could be shown that Bonaparte died of a diseased liver, then his prolonged detention at St Helena and those who enforced it could be held, at least in part, to blame. All the English doctors at once agreed that the cause of death was cancer of the stomach. But when the liver was examined, Dr Shortt, the principal medical officer at St Helena, was alone in considering it enlarged. He stuck to his opinion, though in the end he, with three of his colleagues, signed the final report that spoke of disease within the stomach. The liver, the report said, in deference to Shortt's view, was 'perhaps a little larger than natural'. Antommacchi did not sign the report, a fact which later lent strength to the rumours that there had been irregular and dark dealings at Longwood that day. In fact, he refrained from signing at Bertrand's insistence because the report referred only to the body of Napoleon Bonaparte and not to 'the Emperor' – a reminder that this cursed and futile quarrel over titles and methods of address extended beyond life into death.

When Lowe received the report, he objected to the description of the liver, and the offending words were then excised from the final version. Lowe's insistence on this excision cannot fail to invite grave suspicion. Did the Governor's anxiety over his own conduct and reputation extend to browbeating his own medical officer? The answer would seem to be yes, and it is no credit to Shortt that he tamely agreed (though he did keep the report's original, with the annotation, in his own hand, 'the words obliterated were suppressed by the orders of Sir Hudson Lowe'.)[8] On the other hand, the confusion and conflicting evidence about the autopsy and its aftermath are such that firm judgements and apportionment of blame are not as clear cut as a first perusal of the facts would seem to justify. For example, Shortt, writing to his brother-in-law in Scotland the very next day, 7 May, appeared to have changed his mind, claiming that the liver was perfectly sound: 'had he been on the throne of France instead of an inhabitant of St Helena, he would equally have suffered, as no earthly power could have cured the disease [cancer of the stomach] when formed.'[9]

Napoleon had said in his will that he wished to be buried in Paris 'by the banks of the Seine and among the French whom I have loved so well'. More precisely, he wanted to lie in the Père Lachaise cemetery in Paris (nowhere near the Seine) between the tombs of Masséna and Lefebvre. No conceivable British or French government could allow this. As Rosebery succinctly put it: 'the arrival of the dead Napoleon in Europe would have been second only in embarrassment to the arrival of the living.'[10] Bonaparte also said that if he must remain in the island, he would wish to be buried in the so-called Vale of

Geranium, close to where two willow trees grew and where a freshwater spring had supplied Longwood.

But before the funeral, there was in fact if not in name the lying-in-state. And before that, the rush to create a likeness of the dead man's features, a rush in which Arnott and Dr Burton, another of the signatories to the autopsy report, represented, as it were, England. Arnott, the Governor's nominee in the death chamber, tried on the night of 5 May, but without success, to get an impression of the face by pressing into it a lump of softened candlewax. Antommacchi was also unsuccessful with some rough plaster. Burton was the most ingenious. He prepared a fine white powder, though it is not clear whether this was from crushed crystals which with some difficulty he had procured from a neighbouring island or from pounding up plaster figurines he had bought in Jamestown, the capital. All this took time. It was not until 7 May, when Bonaparte had been dead for forty hours, that Burton succeeded in getting one mould of his face and another of the back of his head. He then took casts of the moulds. He was only just in time; decomposition was beginning to set in. Disappointingly for him, he did not manage to retain all his handiwork. The mask of the face was carried off by the determined Mme Bertrand, leaving Burton with only that of the back of the skull. Years later, Antommacchi, who had been allowed by Mme Bertrand to take a copy of 'her' prize, attempted with some success but no truth whatever, to claim that he was responsible for making the mask.

Before the body had begun to decompose, it was laid out, dressed in the green uniform of a colonel of the Chasseurs of the Guard and laid on the richly embroidered cloak that Bonaparte had worn at the Battle of Marengo. Then, on the evening of 6 May, the public was allowed in to pay homage, or to satisfy its curiosity, or both. The officers of the two British regiments came first (the 20th and the 66th), then the NCOs, then the ships' companies from the naval vessels and finally the civilians of the island. The process went on for two days. It was almost a repeat performance of the crowds at Torbay six years before, except that this time there were obviously no shouts or cheering, only bowed heads and respectful silence. One soldier, leading his little son by the hand, told the child: 'take a good look at Napoleon, he is the greatest man in the world.'[11] According to Montholon, officers of the Royal Navy 'entreated to be allowed the honour of pressing their lips to the cloak of Marengo'. One British officer, having seen the body, wrote: 'we may now safely say he was one of the greatest conquerors this world has ever produced, but not a great and noble character'.[12] Bertrand records that the majority of people touched Napoleon's hand.[13]

On the evening of 7 May the body was lowered into the innermost of four coffins in which it was finally enclosed. George Rutledge, a junior surgeon who had attended the autopsy and who had watched over the corpse, rather cheekily scratched his name, 'as being the last British officer who had ever seen the deceased', on a small metal plate, which he added to the other objects being placed within the coffin. There was a last-minute argument about Napoleon's heart. At the autopsy, just before the body was closed up, Montholon announced that the deceased had wanted his heart sent to Marie-Louise, his wife. Pending the Governor's ruling, it was put into a small silver cup and handed to Rutledge for safekeeping. The indefatigable Mme Bertrand tried to get it from him, but in the end it was placed, together with the stomach, in the coffin.

Meanwhile, the grave had been dug by men of the Corps of Engineers. Covered with the Marengo cloak, the heavy multiple coffin was borne from Longwood by twelve soldiers from the 20th Regiment to an improvised hearse. At every stage of the journey to the graveside, full ceremonial honours were accorded. The entire garrison of the island, 3,000 in all, manned the route with arms reversed, specially composed music was played by a military band, warships in the harbour fired salutes, and a shore battery responded. At the final steep approach to the grave, teams of soldiers and naval ratings, working in relays, carried the coffin from its hearse down to the graveside. As it was lowered into the ground, three salvos of fifteen rounds were fired by the artillery. After it was all over, there was a sudden rush of the waiting crowds of soldiers and civilians towards the willow trees, from which they stripped branches and twigs as souvenirs. To prevent this from happening again, Lowe gave orders that the grave should be protected by railings – the very railings which had been installed around the new Longwood, and which had caused Bonaparte to say that he would never enter the building as long as they were there. A military guard was mounted to watch over the tomb. One of the members of this guard, evidently the NCO, wrote to his mother how 'I have a sentry promenading on each side of [the grave] to catch him if he gets up'.[14]

It was this same soldier who, given permission to take time off from his duties at the grave, went to Longwood to see for himself where and how the ex-Emperor had lived – one more example of how Bonaparte, alive or dead, excited never-ceasing curiosity. This cheery soul went so far as to try on one of the dead man's hats. 'He must have had an extraordinary wide head, for it would not fit me when put on square (the way he always wore it),' he wrote. The soldier, incidentally, found Longwood in a wretched state: he told his mother that 'I could not have lived as he did, I am sure, half the time he did'.[15]

Lowe also went to Longwood, and so did Lady Lowe, as curious as everyone else. One of the documents awaiting examination was Bonaparte's will, in which he took one last swipe at the English – or at least at their chosen representatives. 'I am dying prematurely,' he had written (he composed his last will between 15 and 26 April, two weeks before his death), 'murdered by the English oligarchy and its hired assassins [i.e. Lowe] ... The English nation will avenge my death before long.' At about the same time, he had said much the same thing to Arnott:

> That is the hospitality of your government ... I have been murdered piecemeal and with premeditation ... Hudson Lowe had made himself the executioner of the capital sentence of your ministers ... you will end like the proud Republic of Venice, and as for me, dying on this ghastly rock, I bequeath the disgrace of my death to the Royal family of England.[16]

In another, particularly spiteful expression of anti-British feeling, Bonaparte in his will left 10,000 francs to Cantillon, the man who had tried to murder the Duke of Wellington in Paris in February 1818. He was inexplicably acquitted by a French jury, and Bonaparte wrote in the will that 'he had just as much right to assassinate this oligarch as the latter had to send me to perish on the rock of St Helena ... Cantillon, if he had really killed the Lord, would have been justified by the same motives, the interest of France'.

The news of the ex-Emperor's death, once it became public knowledge in Britain, provoked mixed reactions, in which acknowledgement of his 'greatness' vied with recollections of his ruthless conquests. The Annual Register for 1821 allowed itself the unaccustomed luxury of editorial judgement, writing of Napoleon as having long been the 'scourge of France and made her the scourge of Europe'. But the writer then goes on to describe this 'wonderful man' and his 'terrific career of blood and power and destruction and guilt; no human being ever gave more unequivocal proofs of commanding genius'. He

> placed himself at the head of the armies of a people among whom he was a stranger, thence to exalt himself into their acknowledged sovereign; to put an end to the anarchy whose long continuance had worn them out; to restore internal tranquillity to the nation, while he placed it in a state of

permanent war with the whole world; to destroy the armies and overturn the thrones of the surrounding princes; and to make his will the law of the continent of Europe.

All this, the author declares, afforded 'incontrovertible proofs of superlative genius'.

Blackwood's *Edinburgh Magazine* was a great deal less complimentary in its issue of July 1821. The editorialist admitted that Napoleon was 'a man of great military talents', but he showed a complete lack of political wisdom in supposing he could conquer England, which was always so much stronger than France. 'If there had been a highway from Dover to Calais five-and-twenty years ago, Waterloo would have been anticipated by five-and-twenty years.' After that blast on Britannia's trumpet, the writer gets down to some vigorous demonising of Napoleon. He was 'selfish, perfidious, bloody ... he had no value for any life but his own ... he crushed the hope of freedom in France and would have crushed it throughout the world ... a tyrant in the darkest sense of the name ... adulterer, apostate ... declared an outlaw by all nations ... after having run the career of a villain, he died the death of a slave'. Elsewhere in the magazine, it is recorded that seventeen readers submitted contributions in prose and verse on the death of Bonaparte. Two of the poems are printed, neither of them of much merit, but both striking a kindlier, less abusive note than that sounded by the editorial. Both make the point that this is no time to be dancing on a dead man's grave. As the second of the two poems puts it:

> Shame to the bard who would raise his voice
> One hostile feeling to cherish,
> Shame to the Briton that dare rejoice
> When the fallen and mighty perish.

A similar spirit of pity and respect is expressed by a letter-writer to the *Morning Chronicle* of 9 July 1821. This person is far from giving Napoleon a clean bill of health; on the contrary he is described as being filled 'with a wild and selfish ambition'. But the writer links him in villainy with Castlereagh (by now Lord Londonderry) for the latter's role in 'betraying the liberties of Europe' – i.e. in helping to restore the old, monarchical order that Napoleon had sought to destroy. The letter concludes, rather pompously, that despots are not only royal and military but civil and military as well: 'whether Napoleon, on his distant and deserted death bed, or the Marquis of Londonderry, in the business and bustle of his official life, have been nearly as equal in their repentance as in their guilt, is not likely ever to be known.'

As was to be expected, Lord Holland, no less than his wife, was shocked by the news of Bonaparte's death, and immediately settled down in his Paris lodgings 'to transcribe some hasty and rambling notes taken when the news of his death reached me'. More than a hundred pages of these notes are encompassed in Holland's *Foreign Reminiscences*, a work published nearly thirty years later. He admits to having had very little personal contact with Napoleon, and so his notes are based on conversations with and recollections of those who did know him. The whole account is therefore more a résumé of what other people, mostly French, knew and remembered of Napoleon than the personal appraisal of one Englishman prone to defend Napoleon. Holland does, however, express one or two personal views. Like almost everyone in England, and many in France, he considers that the execution of the Duc d'Enghien 'will and ought to remain a blot upon Napoleon's memory'. He also vigorously rejects the stories put about by 'our ignorant libellists' alleging dissoluteness at the Imperial court; on the contrary, says Holland, 'his court, if not the most refined and agreeable, was the least immoral and dissipated known in France for three centuries'.

He further observes that Napoleon, even at the height of his powers, seldom resorted to revenge against those who displeased him; 'of what man possessed of such extended yet such disputed authority, can so much be said? Of Washington, of

Cromwell?' Never in France 'was justice more steadily and equally administered between man and even between government and its subjects', although Holland has the honesty to admit – he could scarcely have done otherwise – that 'the principles of freedom, which can alone secure good institutions from abuse, were nearly extinguished under his absolute rule'. In conclusion, Holland writes that Napoleon's life is 'more interesting and more instructive to posterity than that of any great military prince since Julius Caesar'.

One other point made in these notes concerns Hudson Lowe, who at one stage (see p. 45) was an habitué of Holland House. Sir Neil Campbell, writes Holland, was 'overwhelmed with surprise' at the Emperor's escape from Elba, where Campbell was supposed to be responsible for preventing just such an escape. 'The ridicule to which his want of vigilance exposed him had a pernicious effect afterwards on the nerves of Sir Hudson Lowe which led to that officer adopting a system more irksome to his great prisoner and more discreditable to England than even the narrow policy of our councils had intended.' The words show that Holland remained unshaken in his beliefs, first expounded in the House of Lords in 1817, that an irreparable wrong had been perpetrated by Lord Liverpool's government in its decision to send Napoleon to St Helena and in its treatment of him there.

Meanwhile, Bonaparte slept on beneath the willow trees. The Longwood group returned to Europe, as did Sir Hudson and Lady Lowe. But if anyone supposed that the memory of the former Emperor, at least in British minds, would die away with the passing of the years, they were massively mistaken. In 1822 O'Meara's resounding act of revenge, in the form of his *Napoleon in Exile, a Voice from St Helena*, appeared; and four years later a gigantic (nine octavo volumes) life of the most famous man in Europe by the most famous writer in Europe was published. Sir Walter Scott was paid the unheard-of advance of 10,500 guineas (about £525,000 at today's value) for his labour, undertaken in order to meet the claims of his creditors after his bankruptcy.

'They say,' records Bertrand in his diary on 12 May 1821, a few days after the funeral, 'that the body of the Emperor will not remain there for long.' Whoever 'they' might have been, they had an extraordinary gift of prophecy.*

---

*Even in death, Bonaparte was denied proper designation. Montholon wanted the white slabs covering the grave to be inscribed '*NAPOLEON, né à Ajaccio le 15 Août 1769, mort à St Hélène le 5 Mai 1821*'. Lowe insisted that after Napoleon should come the word 'Bonaparte'. Montholon objected, and so the stone bore no inscription at all.

5

Soul of Evil or Greatest Man?

With Napoleon dead but not forgotten, the time has come to examine the attitudes towards him of contemporary poets and men of letters, not just in the shadow of his death but more generally. As might be expected, these attitudes varied and were often contradictory. Byron is a particularly striking example of someone whose opinions veered sharply from one direction to another. Nor is this surprising. He was notoriously ambivalent about many things. On one side, Napoleon's enemies – the old monarchies, Castlereagh, Metternich, etc., were also the poet's *bêtes noires*. On the other, his appreciation of liberty and his hostility towards despotism in all its forms landed him in a quagmire of divided loyalties. As the odds against Napoleon shortened and he faced defeat, Byron told his journal that he would not mind his hero being beaten by 'men', but not by 'three stupid boobies of regular bred sovereigns [George III and the Emperors of Russia and Austria]'.[1]

While still a schoolboy at Harrow, the future poet had to defend a bust of his hero 'against the rascally time-servers', supporters of Pitt and others who brought the Peace of Amiens to an end. He wrote in his journal (27 November 1813) that 'He [Napoleon] has been a *Héro de Roman* of mine' on the Continent, but added significantly 'I don't want him here'. As was inevitable with contemporaries assessing Napoleon's policies, character and achievements, Byron, who was born only a year before the outbreak of the French Revolution, was faced with the double and contrasting vision of the Emperor as the heir to that revolution, the destroyer of the old order, the bringer of light and liberty, and Napoleon the despot, the imperial megalomaniac, the squanderer of his soldiers' lives. In 'The Age of Bronze', written two years after Napoleon's death, the poet gives voice to this ambiguity:

> Yes, where is he, the champion and the child
> of all that's great or little, wise or wild,
> whose games were empires and whose stakes were thrones,
> whose table earth, whose dice were human bones?
> Behold the great result, in yon lone isle,
> And, as thy nature urges, weep or smile.
> Sigh to behold the eagle's lofty rage
> Reduced to nibble at his narrow cage,
> Smile to survey the queller of the nations,
> Now daily squabbling o'er disputed rations.

(The last lines evidently refer to the stories, circulated by O'Meara on his return from St Helena, about allegedly inadequate provisions at Longwood.)

Yet in the same poem there are lines extolling Napoleon's memory and stature:

> The rocky isle that holds or held his dust
> shall crown the Atlantic like the hero's bust[2]

or again:

> O heaven! of which he was a power and feature,
> O earth! of which he was a noble creature.

Byron, predictably, manages a thrust at Sir Hudson Lowe, who had refused to allow a full, Imperial, inscription on Napoleon's coffin:

> What though his gaoler, dutious to the last

124

scarced deemed the coffin's lead could keep him fast,
refusing one poor line along the lid
to date the birth and death of all it hid.

Byron's characteristically muddled thinking about ideal forms of government is given free rein in his journal for November 1813, where he comments on Napoleon's waning star:

> I thought, if crushed, he would have fallen ... and not have been pared away to gradual insignificance ... here we are, retrograding to the dull, stupid old system – balance of Europe – poising straws upon kings' noses, instead of wringing them off. Give me a republic, or a despotism of one, rather than the mixed government of one, two, or three'.

What this passage suggests is that Byron was particularly upset by the spectacle of Napoleon's conduct in defeat. Instead of ignominiously surrendering, he should have gone in some sort of (unspecified) blaze of glory. 'Ah, my poor little Pa-god, Napoleon has walked off his pedestal. He has abdicated, they say ... I cannot bear such a crouching catastrophe.'[3] In his journal for the same day, he records that he is 'utterly bewildered and confounded ... alas, this imperial diamond hath a flaw in it, and is now hardly fit to stick in a glazier's pencil'. Despite what has happened, Byron 'won't give him up, though all his admirers have'. Equally regrettable (this is after the first abdication), Napoleon's fall has brought 'the restoration of the despicable Bourbons' and the 'utter wreck of a mind which I thought superior even to fortune' (letter to Annabelle Milbanke, 20 April 1814). In other words, what Byron really minded was not so much Napoleon's going as the manner of his going:

> . . . but yesterday a King
> and armed with Kings to strive
> and now thou art a nameless thing:
> so abject – yet alive!
>   ('Ode to Napoleon Bonaparte')

Soon after the Battle of Waterloo, one of Napoleon's carriages, captured by the Austrians at Jemappes, was brought to London and put on show in Piccadilly. Immense crowds came to see it – further proof that to the English, curiosity rather than admiration (one can easily admire a person, less easily a vehicle) was the prevailing attitude towards the defeated Emperor. Whether Byron was among the crowds we cannot know, but what is certain is that he commissioned Charles Baxter, a well-known coachmaker in Long Acre, to build for his own use a replica of the carriage. The Napoleonic conveyance, according to one of the poet's friends,[4] was enormous: 'standing rather high ... it was painted dark blue with a blue border and the imperial arms on the doors. Inside, drawers and compartments were fitted for every conceivable utensil for a Napoleonic campaign and these were to be replaced in Byron's version by a bed, a library and every apparatus for dining.' What Byron thought he was doing in ordering such a monstrous affair can only be guessed at. He was heavily in debt at the time. One tentative explanation[5] is that he was thinking of driving in his great wagon to Paris, where he would contribute, in some undefined way, to the 'liberation' of France from the Bourbons. In the event, he shipped the vehicle to Venice when he went into exile in 1816. The real story of the carriage remains a mystery, but it seems impossible to dismiss the thought that in commissioning it Byron was indulging in the fantasy that he was, in some supernatural way, the counterpart and spiritual brother, or perhaps cousin, of Napoleon. The theory is lent strength by the stanza in the eleventh canto of 'Don Juan':

> Even I – albeit I'm sure I did not know it
> Nor sought of foolscap subjects to be king,
> Was reckoned, a considerable time,
> The Grand Napoleon of rhyme.

Annabelle Milbanke, Byron's unhappy wife, echoed the same thought when she wrote 'he is the absolute monarch of words, and uses them, as Bonaparte did lives, for conquest'.

The effect on Byron of Napoleon's second abdication and surrender was such as to call into question his sanity. Annabelle Milbanke, whom he had married in January 1815, left him a year later, believing that he was suffering from hydrocephalus (water on the brain). His friend Hobhouse wrote that while Bonaparte was at Plymouth 'Byron confesses that he sometimes thinks there is nothing left for it but to follow Whitbread's example [i.e. to commit suicide; see p. 29]'. There were similar outbreaks of romantic agony among Napoleon's admirers at the news of his death. Hobhouse recorded in his diary for 1822, a year later, that 'both my body and my mind have undergone a change for the worse in the last year ... I feel confident I shall not live much longer, so what I intend to do in the world, I must do quickly'. This proved to be a singularly inaccurate prophecy, seeing that Hobhouse, ennobled as Lord Broughton, lived for another forty-seven years. Elizabeth Inchbald, the actress and playwright, admirer of Fox and above all of Napoleon, had taken to her bed at the first abdication, and did so again on hearing of Napoleon's death; within a month she was dead from intestinal troubles.

If Byron was ambivalent about Napoleon, he was not alone among the poets. Coleridge, twenty years his senior, had in his youth been a devotee of Fox; he had greeted the fall of the Bastille with an enthusiastic ode in which – he was only sixteen – he recorded the 'Universal cry of liberty echoing from Gallia's shore'. As for Bonaparte, the poet began by hoping, like Fox, that he would turn out to be another Washington, and believed (1799) that he was sincere in seeking peace. But before long, Coleridge's articles for the *Morning Post* and *The Courier* began to sound a note increasingly hostile to the Corsican, to the point where the always impressionable and self-centred poet came to believe that Bonaparte was bent on personal revenge against him as he travelled in Italy. As he warmed to the task of excoriating his enemy, Coleridge justified his attitude by 'the necessity of ever refuelling the moral feelings of the people as to the monstrosity of the giant fiend that menaces them'.[6] By

1811 he was writing that 'the death of Bonaparte would be the greatest blessing by which any human event could at present befall mankind'. In a series of satirical articles for *The Courier*, he discussed the idea of whether it was politically, morally and ethically right to assassinate Napoleon, the architect of 'the greatest tyranny that every scourged mankind'.

What happened was that the French Republic, after its dramatic over-turning of old gods, had evolved into an empire. In doing so, it and Bonaparte had lost for ever the earlier admiration of Coleridge and others of his literary contemporaries. This complete if gradual change of heart may account in part for Coleridge's failure, despite encouragement by publishers and editors, to embark on a 'Character of Bonaparte'. Had he ever done so, it would have been, beyond all doubt, antagonistic, just as the essay on Pitt, if ever written, would have been. Napoleon's defeat, banishment and death seem not greatly to have affected Coleridge. By that time, he had, after years of being a slave to opium, emerged as a sage, surrounded by a following of disciples. The Jacobinism of his youth lay in the past, long forgotten.

Coleridge's great friend and fellow visionary, Wordsworth, shared a similar experience of disillusionment. An early admiration for the French Revolution is expressed in the oft-quoted lines from 'The Prelude':

> Bliss was it in that dawn to be alive,
> But to be young was very heaven.

They reflect the young poet's exhilaration as, during a long visit to France in 1791–2, in order to learn French, he talked over revolutionary ideas with his French friend Michel Beaupuy.*

*As well as learning French, Wordsworth fell in love with a French girl, Annette Vallon, who bore him a daughter, Caroline. Ten years later, in the summer of 1802 (during the peace created by the Treaty of Amiens), Wordsworth, accompanied by his sister Dorothy, was back in Paris, explaining to Annette that he was going to marry Mary Hutchinson.

But his enthusiasm began to wane when faced with the horror of the September (1792) massacres in Paris and the victory of Robespierre and the Jacobins over the more moderate Girondins, with whom Wordsworth felt a natural affinity. Thus were sown the seeds of his later conservatism and his hatred and mistrust of mob rule. But it was not until ten years later, as the young Bonaparte was being installed as Consul for life, that Wordsworth began to assume the mantle of the patriot, the defender of liberty against the despotic threat presented by Napoleonic France. It was this attitude which gave birth to such lines as 'Vanguard of liberty, ye men of Kent' from the series of poems grouped under the title of 'National Independence and Liberty', themselves calls to arms and appeals to Englishmen to prepare themselves by moral regeneration for the coming struggle.

Bonaparte's so-called Act of Mediation (1803), which followed the challenge to Swiss independence by a French military invasion, brought Switzerland completely under his control. Wordsworth wrote to his Cambridge friend James Losh: 'after Bonaparte had violated the independence of Switzerland, my heart turned against him and against the nation that could submit to be the instrument of such an outrage'. From that moment onwards, until the final fall of Napoleon, Wordsworth's mind was dominated by the need to defeat France and its ruler. The 'National Independence and Liberty' poems bear witness to this patriotic fervour. They include the sonnets, 'I grieved for Buonaparté [sic]', in which the poet wonders about the contents of the First Consul's mind, the one about the French domination of Switzerland, with its reference to 'the Tyrant', and no. XXII, which includes the lines:

> I see one man, of men the meanest too,
> raised up to sway the world, to do, undo
> with the mighty nations for his underlings.

These works were written in 1802–1803, but despite their

129

power as poetic utterance 'there is no evidence that the world took much notice of them'.[7] Three years later, Napoleon's defeat of the Prussians at the Battle of Jena (1806) inspired the sonnet beginning:

> Another year! another deadly blow!
> Another mighty empire overthrown!
> And we are left, or shall be left, alone;
> The last that dare to struggle with the foe.

The allied victory at Waterloo and the defeat of Napoleon undammed a stream of poems – sonnets and odes – in which the fallen Emperor is described as

> That soul of Evil which, from Hell let loose,
> had filled the astonished world with such abuse
> as boundless patience could endure

who had waged war 'with desperate mind/against the life and virtue of mankind'. Hatred of foreign tyranny, love of national independence and freedom, and fear of what 'the mob' might do were the three channels along which Wordsworth's political thinking flowed. Given this, his detestation of Napoleon and all he stood for was as inevitable as sunrise or the cycle of the seasons.

Because he supported the war against France did not mean that the poet approved of Lord Liverpool and his government. Neither he nor Southey ever became deferential Tories. Nor had he any respect for the ideas of Holland House and those who 'would crouch to a sanguinary tyrant'.[8] His ideas on international affairs were summed up in his pamphlet on the Convention of Cintra (1808), the agreement by which French troops defeated by Wellington's armies in Portugal were to be transported back to France in British ships (and therefore made available once more to Napoleon). This, Wordsworth maintained, showed a complete lack of respect for the Spanish and Portuguese national resistance movements. The Spanish war was, for him, a political and national affair, involving none the less the fate of all nations, indeed of humanity itself: 'the Spaniards are instruments of benefit and glory for the human race.' Wordsworth was ready to allow that, though Napoleonic armies were 'a branded multitude of perfidious oppressors',[9] they were also, like Napoleon himself, the children 'of noble peasants, Liberty and Philanthropic laws'. The Cintra tract, according to A.V. Dicey, who had it reprinted in 1915 in order that British resolve in the war against Germany might be strengthened, helped to arouse public enthusiasm for the conflict with Napoleon: 'it immediately brought into line every man throughout the United Kingdom who detested the despotism of Bonaparte.' If true, this would be significant evidence of anti-Napoleonic feelings. But Dicey's claim is a claim only, unsupported by any proof.[10]

Robert Southey, a minor star compared with the planetary brilliance of Wordsworth or Coleridge (the latter was his brother-in-law), went through the same process of dis-illusionment over France as they had. As a radical would-be re-former who had collaborated with Coleridge in planning a 'pantisocracy' in America – a sort of early kibbutz movement where all property and tasks would be shared in common – he sympathised with the original aims of the Revolution and wrote a poem, 'Joan of Arc', to celebrate the event. 'Old things seemed passing away,' he wrote years later to his friend Caroline Bowles, 'and nothing was dreamt of but the regeneration of the human race.'[11]

But this exalted mood soon passed; the execution of Girondins in 1793 dismayed Southey, as it had Wordsworth. Napoleon's assumption of power and the growth of ambition completed Southey's conversion. Unlike many other initial critics of Napoleon, he seems not to have fallen, however reluc-tantly they fell, under the spell cast by the 'genius' or 'super-man'; on the contrary, he saw the Emperor as a demonic force, describing in his poem 'The Curse of Kehema' (1810) an avaricious ruler with his eyes fixed not only on domination on earth but in heaven and hell as well. Coleridge, in his articles for *The Courier*, argued similarly that Napoleon was not just a despot but the incarnation of evil, the enemy of all mankind.

Southey in 1809 became one of the founders of and a regular contributor to the *Quarterly Review*, the organ of orthodox Toryism. But it was the French incursion into Spain and Portugal and the resistance mounted against it that marked the real turning-point – or act of apostasy, according to one's outlook – in the attitudes of one-time pro-Revolutionaries towards France and Napoleon. Southey, for example, who had until then been highly critical of the government's conduct of the war, now described the British army as 'the single plank between us and the Red Sea of an English Jacquerie',[12] a sentiment that expressed his deep-seated fear that French excesses might spread to England. Southey's line of thought had been foreshadowed earlier by both Wordsworth and Southey himself, when, partly under the influence of Burke, they adopted frankly reactionary hostility towards domestic reforms, lest they should lead to the establishment of a Napoleonic tyranny in England. As for Napoleon himself, the invasion of Spain was for Southey 'the first instance in which [he] unequivocally displayed himself in his true character of pure devil'.[13]

Holding such views, Southey cannot have agreed with the sentiments expressed to him by the poet and essayist Charles Lamb in August 1815: 'Bonaparte is a fine fellow, as my barber says, and I should not mind standing bare-headed at his table to do him service in his fall. They should have given him Hampton Court or Kensington, with a tether extending to 40 miles round London.' Was Lamb joking? He had a reputation for eccentric witticisms. Thackeray once called him 'St Charles ... while looking at one of his half-mad letters and remembering his devotion to his half-mad sister'.[14]

Shelley, the eternal rebel, whose 'philosophy is pure revolt, unqualified by a single saving clause of common sense',[15] was born three years after the onset of the French Revolution. He was in no position, therefore, to go through the disillusioning process experienced by the older Romantic poets over the descent of the French Revolutionaries into violence and terror. But he nevertheless had the profoundest contempt for Napoleon as tyrant. Writing in stinging terms to his friend Thomas Jefferson Hogg in December 1812, when he was aged twenty, he described Bonaparte as

> a person to whom I have a very great objection; he is to me a hateful and despicable human being. He is seduced by the grossest and most vulgar ambition into actions which only differ from those of pirates by virtue of the number of men and the variety of resources under his command. His talents appear to be altogether contemptible and commonplace; incapable as he is of comparing connectedly the most obvious propositions, or relish any pleasure truly enrapturing. Excepting Lord Castlereagh, you could not have mentioned any character but Bonaparte whom I condemn and abhor more violently.[16]

Shelley devoted a poem to the defeat of Napoleon in 1815 ('Feelings of a Republican on the Fall of Bonaparte'), which included the line 'I hated thee, fallen tyrant' but which also recognised that the disappearance of the dictator did not automatically signify the restoration of liberty:

> I know too late, since thou and France are in the dust,
> That virtue owes a more eternal foe
> Than Force or Fraud: old custom, legal crime
> And bloody faith and foulest birth of time.

Six years later (1821) the poet was reflecting on Napoleon's death:

> Napoleon's fierce spirit rolled
> in terror and blood and gold
> A torrent of rain to death from his birth
> leave the millions who follow to mould

the metal before it be cold;
And weave into his shame, which like the dead
shrouds me, the hopes that from his glory fled.

One contemporary who never wavered in his admiration of Napoleon, not simply as the residuary legatee of the Revolution but as the champion of freedom, was William Hazlitt, artist, poet, essayist and journalist. Not for him the apostasy, the second thoughts and recantations of Wordsworth, Coleridge or Southey. Anyone who succeeded in overthrowing stupid monarchs with the panache that characterised Napoleon's campaigns was a hero in Hazlitt's eyes. A true radical, he could easily have composed the line 'A mortal man beyond all mortal praise', which was in fact the work of Walter Savage Landor, originally another idoliser of Napoleon – except that he, Landor, subsequently joined the ranks of the turncoats. As John Bailey, reviewing a book about Hazlitt's literary style in *The Times* (9 July 1998), put it: '[his] enthusiasm for Napoleon is all of the piece with his radicalism and goes with that half-conscious worship of political power in a new exciting form which had made an ardent republican into a Napoleon worshipper, and which in our own time has seen the Left secretly or openly in love with dictators such as Stalin.'

Hazlitt's joyous reaction to the news of Napoleon's victory at Austerlitz stands out in sharp contrast with the gloomy prospect foreseen by most of his countrymen: 'I walked out in the evening, and as I returned saw the evening star set over a poor man's cottage, with other thoughts and feelings than I shall never have again.' The inference here is that Napoleon's ever-rising star is also the star of hope for the poor cottager. It is small wonder that Hazlitt, feeling as he did, was utterly cast down by the final defeat of the Emperor. Thomas Talfourd, Charles Lamb's first biographer, gives a vivid description of meeting Hazlitt for the first time in 1815, when he was 'staggering under the blow of Waterloo ... the reappearance of his imperial idol on the coast of France, and his triumphal

march to Paris, like a fairy vision, had excited his admiration
and sympathy to the utmost pitch; and though in many respects
sturdily English in feeling, he could scarcely forgive the valour
of the conquerors; and bitterly resented the captivity of the
Emperor in St Helena, which followed it, as if he had sustained
a personal wrong'.[17] B.R. Haydon's diaries paint a similar
picture of the afflicted writer. 'It is not to be believed how that
destruction of Napoleon affected him; he seemed prostrated in
mind and body, he walked about unwashed, unshaved, hardly
sober by day, and always intoxicated by night, literally, without
exaggeration, for weeks; until at length, wakening up as if it
were from his stupor, he at once left off all the stimulating
liquors, and never touched them after.'[18] Hazlitt's own account
of his state of mind over Napoleon's defeat was written later, in
his *Journey through France and Italy* (1826): 'and with him all
we who remained were thrown into the pit, the lifeless bodies
of men, and wore round our necks the collars of servitude and
on our foreheads the brand, and in our souls the stain of
thraldom and of the born slaves of Kings.'

Hazlitt's final tribute to his hero was his four-volume *Life of
Napoleon Bonaparte*, the first two volumes published in 1827,
the remaining two in 1830, not long before his own death. The
timing was unfortunate; Scott's enormous biography had
appeared in 1827 and received greater acclaim (and greater
sales). Poor Hazlitt's efforts gained him nothing financially. The
publishers had promised him a £500 advance but went bank-
rupt; all he got in the end was a (dud) bill for £140.[19] The most
interesting aspect of this long-forgotten work is to be found in
the (unpublished) preface, where he seeks to explain why he
wrote the book. His first aim was to exalt Napoleon as someone
who stood between the legitimate kings and their habitual
victims – mankind. He continued:

> There were two other feelings that influenced me – a love of
> glory, when it did not interfere with other things, and wish to
> see personal merit prevail over external rank and circumstance.

> I felt pride (not envy) to think that there was one reputation in modern times equal to the ancients, and at seeing one man greater than the throne he sat upon.

The cautious publishers, to Hazlitt's indignation, considered this preface too contentious.

The reaction to Napoleon's downfall of William Cobbett, ex-soldier, super-patriotic Englishman, vigorous pamphleteer, defender of rural values and opponent of industrialisation, does not fit neatly into a pro- or anti-Napoleon frame. He was very far, it is true, from being an admirer: in a conversation in Philadelphia in 1796 with Talleyrand, then in exile, he said, with a flash of inspiration, that 'I should not be at all surprised to see even this newly-fledged cut-throat finish his career by wearing the crown of the Bourbons'.[20] Nor did he, despite his general opposition to the war with France, for a moment wish for or be ready to accept a French victory over England. His inconsistencies over war or no war were themselves a kind of consistency. But when Napoleon's defeat finally brought peace, Cobbett rejoiced, not so much because tyranny had been overthrown – he did not seem to have objected much to Napoleon's dictatorship in France, preferring him to the Bourbons – but because of the prospect (so he hoped) of reform at home and a lowering of taxes. 'The bugbear is gone, the hobgoblin is destroyed. Reason will now resume her sway … the lot of those who do not now live on the taxes must be bettered.'[21] A few months later he was noting that 'the fall of Napoleon is the hardest blow that our taxing system ever felt.'[22]

As this chapter has already suggested, a certain section of British opinion had welcomed the onset of the Revolution in France, none more than William Blake, who in his poem 'The French Revolution' (1791) rejoiced in the coming of a new age of liberty, equality and fraternity. It was the only one of his poems to be published during his lifetime. Its highly imaginative language celebrated the fall of the Bastille and subsequent events in 1789. There is no mistaking the poet's enthusiasm:

> France standing on the top of golden hours
> And human nature seeming born again.

What is significant is that while the work started out as 'The French Revolution, a Poem in seven books', only one, the first, survives. Either Blake, chagrined by developments in France that put an end to his original vision of a dawning golden age, destroyed the other six, or he never wrote them. By the spring of 1815, with Napoleon again on the march, Blake is 'fearful that they will make too great a man of Napoleon, and enable him to come to this country'.[23]

Robert Burns likewise had second thoughts about events in France. His poem 'Does haughty Gaul Invasion Threat', composed in 1795, a year before his death, is an eloquent expression of disappointment. 'As to France,' he wrote in a letter of 5 January 1793 to Robert Graham,[24] 'I was her enthusiastic votary in the beginning of the business ... When she came to show her old avidity for conquest in annexing Savoy etc. to her dominions and invading the rights of Holland, I altered my sentiments.'

But one Englishman whose original Jacobin and pro-Napoleonic faith remained unshaken, save for one aberration, was William Godwin, the philosopher and Shelley's father-in-law. Like so many other radicals of the day, including Wordsworth and Coleridge, Blake and Hazlitt, Godwin came from a Dissenting background, itself the legacy of English seventeenth-century republicanism. Something of a philosophical gasbag, Godwin wrote books and articles – especially 'Poetical Justice' (1793) with its call for a new and better society founded on reason – which had a considerable influence on his contemporaries. Hazlitt in particular rated him highly. Far from being disillusioned by Napoleon's growing ambitions, Godwin saw in him the best hope for the future; 'under his auspicious and beneficent genius', he wrote in 1801,[25] 'everything promises that the future government of France will be popular and her people free'. But by that time, British opinion in general was turning against France and Bonaparte, and Godwin found himself increasingly isolated. Even Sheridan, his friend of earlier days, who had declared the fall of the Bastille to be 'the greatest event that ever happened in the world', changed stance and in 1807 joined the government-of-all-talents, declaring that 'Jacobinism is killed and gone. And by whom? By him who can no longer be called the child and champion of Jacobinism; by Bonaparte.' It was at about this time that 'Political Justice', which had been published at the exorbitant price of three guineas, began changing hands at two shillings a copy.[26]

Godwin, with his hitherto firm but unpopular beliefs, temporarily changed tack when Napoleon embarked on his campaigns against Austria, Prussia, Poland and Spain. Just as he opposed Pitt's war against France on the grounds that no country had the right to interfere in the internal affairs of another, so now he saw Napoleon as an aggressor. But in March 1815, after the Emperor's escape from Elba, Godwin reverted to form in a number of 'open letters' over the signature of 'Verax'.[27] They were published first in the *Morning Post* and then as a pamphlet under his own name. He argued that Napoleon was an important stabilising influence, much to be preferred to the Bourbons. Given his reception in France, he should be recognised as her legitimate ruler, provided he lived in peace with his neighbours. So convinced was he of the soundness of his arguments that Godwin even expressed his hope that in the coming battles Napoleon would carry the day: 'he has expiated his offences and started on a new career ... in a question like this, I feel we cannot succeed and I frankly confess that I do not even wish we should succeed.' This attitude would in any case have met, in the prevailing climate, with scarce response, but as the letters were published only on 22 June, four days after Waterloo, and the date on which Napoleon abdicated, Godwin's suggestions went unheard. That did not deter him from preparing to write a second series of Verax letters under the heading of 'A Dirge of Waterloo', describing the 'miserable consequences of that accursed field'. He even made notes for a life of his hero, though it was never written.[28]

Leigh Hunt, the model for Mr Skimpole in *Bleak House*, founded in 1818 *The Examiner*, a radical weekly review. He was another Napoleonist who used his publication for frequent praise of the Emperor's many talents and his protection of literature, art and science 'which in turn reflected glory on him'. He valued Napoleon's asceticism: 'of fine clothes he does not disguise his contempt', he wrote, apparently unmindful of the pomp and luxury of the Imperial coronation in 1804, or of the stifling etiquette at the court of the Tuileries. On Napoleon's death, *The Examiner*, appearing with a thick black border, editorialised that 'the age has lost its greatest man ... he was far away from our eyes and our thoughts, but we felt a pervading consciousness that he lived and something of a feeling that he might again appear among us ... the news of the event fell upon the town as if it had been a change in the natural world'. But in his autobiography, written years later, Hunt modified considerably his admiration, explaining that he had thought of Napoleon at the time 'as I have thought of him ever since, to wit that he was a great soldier and little else'.

Someone to whom Napoleon became almost an obsession was B.R. Haydon, the painter and endlessly entertaining diarist. Born in 1786, by the age of ten he was reading about Bonaparte, who was to him at once an object of awe and repugnance. He encouraged his little son Harry, who died when not yet four, to venerate Napoleon's memory, and his diaries are full of references, some flattering, some hostile, to his Hero/Daemon. 'He collected unflattering anecdotes about Napoleon to record in his diary, but somehow, as he wrote them down, they always became tinged with admiration of the Emperor's fascination, his audacity, his understanding of human nature, his military genius.'[29] In the diary for 1808, he notes 'after every victory and every exertion of

Bonaparte [Madrid fell to French forces that month] the people of the country console themselves with finding fresh difficulties that must be insurmountable. What man of Genius thinks of difficulties? To indolent asses they may be difficulties, but to Bonaparte only stimulants'.[30] Yet only two years later Haydon was describing in the diary the idyllic view from Primrose Hill, in north London, and reflecting on 'what a change would Bonaparte make in such a scene of liberty and peace – could he but once set his withering foot on this dear land'.[31] In Paris, after the peace of 1814, the painter goes to Gérard's studio and sees the latter's portrait, executed in 1804, of Bonaparte:

> Good God, what a picture. Heavens, a horrid yellow for a complexion, the tip of the nose tinged with red, his eyes a watery, dull, fixed, stern, tiger-like, lurid fierceness; his lips reddish and his mouth cool, collected and resolute. Never in my life do I recollect being so horribly touched … Oh that cruel, bloody, glassy eye, that looked you through without mercy, without feeling'.[32]

Five years later, in December 1819, Haydon confides to his diary that 'Napoleon had done an irreparable injury to liberty by showing the feasibility of complete and systematic despotism'. On 4 July 1821 David Wilkie, his fellow painter, tells him of Napoleon's death:

> Good God! I remember 1805, just after the battle of Jena, we were both groaning at the comparative slowness of our means of acquiring fame, in comparison with him. He is now dead! A captive! And we have gone quietly on rising in daily respect, with no bayonets and cannon to carve our way to fame and honour, and have no cause to lament our silent pathway.[33]

Haydon was not a great painter and certainly not a successful one, specialising in portraits and monumental historical reconstructions as well as in one particular treatment, known as 'musings'. He painted *Wellington Musing on the Field of Waterloo*, began but did not finish *Byron Musing on a Distant*

View of Harrow, and executed no fewer than twenty-three versions of Napoleon musing at St Helena. Other Napoleonic studies, begun but not always finished, included *Napoleon Musing at Fontainebleau Garden*, *Napoleon Musing on the King of Rome* and *Napoleon Musing on the Pyramids at Sunrise*.

The painter, like the majority of English people, had never seen Napoleon, with the result that in some of the versions Haydon made him too fat. Samuel Rogers, the rich banker, poet and collector, commissioned one of these works, in which the artist somewhat thinned down the figure of the former Emperor. The picture, despite its defects, is undeniably compelling. Napoleon, clad in a swallow-tail coat, white breeches and top boots and wearing his famous trade-mark hat, is depicted standing on a clifftop looking out to sea, evidently rapt in thought – musing, in fact. His back is three-quarters turned to the painter, so that only his chin and cheek are visible. In the foreground, a stone at the edge of the cliff bears the inscription '*Ainsi passe la Gloire: Austerlitz, Jena, Wagram, Waterloo*'.

Wordsworth was so taken with the picture that he devoted a sonnet to it, which included the lines:

> And the one man, that laboured to enslave
> the world, sole standing high on the bare hill,
> back turned – arms folded, the unapparent face
> Tinged (we may fancy) in this dreary place
> with light reflected from the invisible sun,
> Set, like his fortunes but not set for aye
> Like them …'

An infinitely greater artist than Haydon also executed a musing kind of portrait of Napoleon. In 1842 J.M.W. Turner painted a rather weird picture of the Emperor at St Helena, entitled *The Exile and the Rock*. It was a companion piece to *Peace: Burial at Sea*, which was Turner's tribute to his friend David Wilkie, who had died on the ship bringing him home from the Middle East and had been buried at sea.

The Napoleon picture showed the captive seen against a visionary landscape, standing on a beach and watched over by a sentry. He in his turn is watching a tiny mollusc, eternally attached to its shell but free, unlike the Emperor, to move wherever and whenever it likes. Turner had a further link with Napoleon, in that he was commissioned to illustrate later editions of Scott's massive *Life*, and in 1832 he went to Brienne, where the young Napoleon had studied at the Military Academy, presumably to acquire local colour.[34]

The Napoleonic Wars came as a godsend to one particular brand of the visual arts. The caricaturists, led by Gillray and followed by Rowlandson and Cruikshank, did as much as anyone to build up the myth (and reality) of the Corsican ogre. They were encouraged by the extraordinary degree of public interest in their output. London print shops, where their work was exhibited, were besieged. 'It is a veritable madness,' wrote a French émigré living in London; 'you have to fight your way in with your fists.'[35] Another foreigner, a German who arrived in London in 1803, confirmed this by observing that an Englishman of fashion doing his daily rounds would first visit Tattersalls, the horse dealers, and then the print shops.[36] At the latter he would find, in 1800, a forerunner to the comic strip, by Gillray, with the general title of *Democracy, or a Life of Bonaparte*. A series of panels illustrated his humble origins, his progress to the First Consulship, which included looting royalist property, the abandonment of his army in Egypt, and finally his lying in bed, tormented by the 'democratic consolations' of ghosts intent on revenge. Also in 1800, Gillray produced a print called *The Apples and the Horse-Turds*, showing Napoleon, as the First Horse-Turd, swimming out to join the Golden Pippins – i.e. the kings and Emperors of Europe. Among the Turds waiting on the bank are various English 'Jacobins', including William Godwin.

The following year – 1801 – Gillray was pressed to embark on another series of Napoleonic crimes but turned down the offer, explaining that 'I fear there will be very little room for Humour

Bonaparte 'musing'. From the painting by B.R Haydon. See page 141.

The death of Bonaparte, 1821. From the painting by Steuben, (Mme Bertrand sitting by the bedside, Count Bertrand in the chair on the left, Dr Antommarchi with hand on pillow, Montholon at foot of bed with outstretched right arm).

Lady Holland. From the painting by Louis Gauffier.

Holland House.

O'Meara.

The exhumation of Bonaparte, 1840.

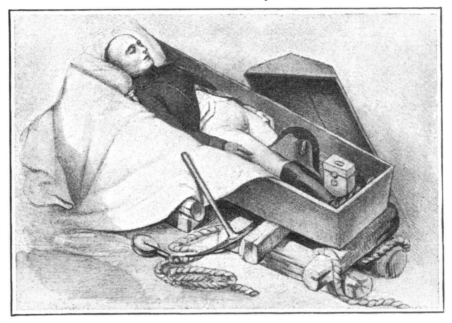

Bonaparte's funeral cortège in the Place de la Concorde.
From the painting by Jacques Guiaud.

The coffin being received in
the church of the Invalides.

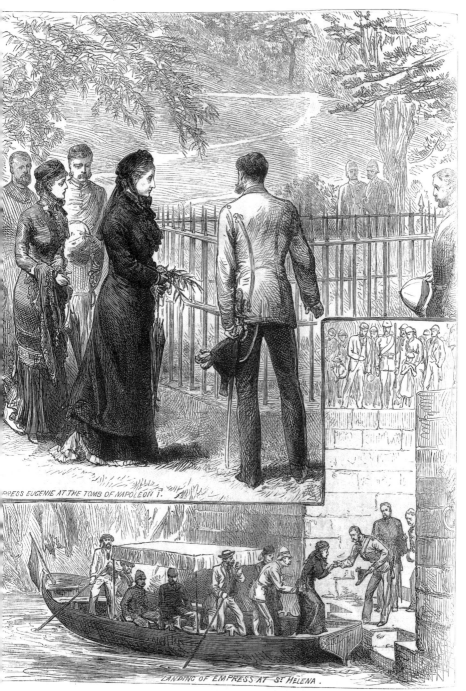

PRESS EUGENIE AT THE TOMB OF NAPOLEON I.

LANDING OF EMPRESS AT ST HELENA.

The Empress Eugénie, widow of Napoleon III, visiting the empty tomb
at St Helena, 1880. See page 183.

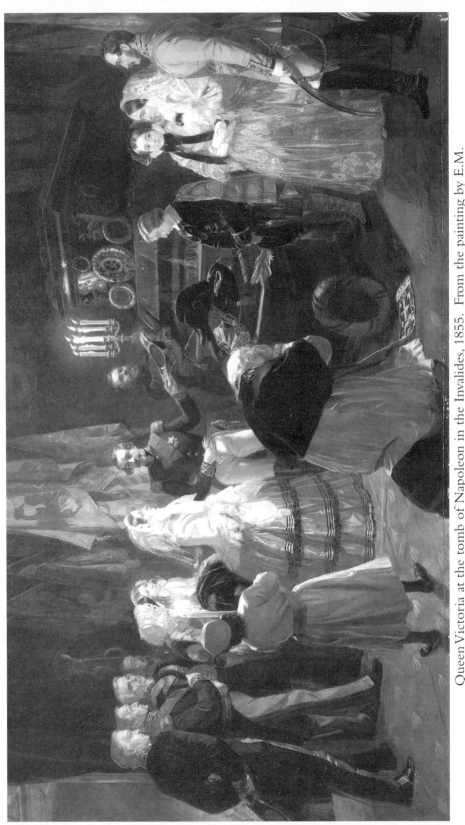

Queen Victoria at the tomb of Napoleon in the Invalides, 1855. From the painting by E.M. Ward RA (Napoleon III beside her, the young Prince of Wales on the right.)

in the life of such a cut-throat'. But with the resumption of the war in 1803, Gillray returned to the task of lampooning Bonaparte. One of his best efforts, *The Plum-Pudding in Danger* (1805), shows Pitt, seated, tall and composed, and Napoleon, small, half-standing, demoniac in countenance, slicing into a huge pudding on the table before them – a reference to the latter's reported suggestion that England and France should share world power.

Gillray, who had begun, like so many of his liberal-minded contemporaries, by sympathising with the aims of the French Revolution and had then reacted sharply and unfavourably to the excesses of 1792–3, continued his campaign against Napoleon until insanity overtook him in 1810. His torch was carried, with equal enthusiasm, by Rowlandson, who exhibited at Ackerman, one of the leading print shops. Caricatures are not supposed or required to be lifelike; their effectiveness depends on grotesque exaggeration and travesty. Rowlandson, who knew France well, excelled at this treatment of the little emperor, ridiculing his vaunted victories, deriding his grandiose declarations, glorying, as the storm clouds of defeat gathered, in his falling fortunes. *The Two Kings of Terror*, executed after his defeat at Leipzig, shows Napoleon dejectedly sitting on a drum, looking into the face of a skeleton, representing death. In the background, half of the French force is attacking; the other is in retreat.

George Cruikshank (who drew the original illustrations for *Oliver Twist*) also found in Napoleon an inexhaustible source of mockery. His caricatures were so popular that they were reproduced on pottery. One such, entitled *Boney, hatching a Bulletin, or Snug Winter Quarters,* is on the theme of the retreat from Moscow. Napoleon, buried up to his neck in snow, is telling his despairing generals, who are asking 'Vat de devil shall we say in de bulletin?' to reply: 'say we shall be home at Xmas for dinner – don't let John Bull know I have been cowpoxed, tell a good lie about the Cossacks. D--- it, tell anything but the truth'. The effect of these outrageous drawings, turned out with great skill and rapidity and displayed to an eager public, who bought them in print form in large numbers, could not fail, as the Napoleonic era drew to a close, to brand as the arch enemy the 'disturber of the peace of Europe'.

Further examples of the lampooning or contempt for Napoleon can be found in the captions that the caricaturists gave to their drawings. They include: the Corsican Monkey, the Corsican Worm, the Corsican Beggar, the Corsican Grasshopper, the Corsican Bloodhound, the Corsican Toad, the Corsican Fox, the Corsican Tiger, the Bonaparte Bear, Crocodile Bonaparte, the Naughty Boy, the Little Man Afraid of His Own Shadow, the Beast of the Apocalypse, Boney quite Mad, Tom Thumb at Bay, the Political Butcher, Napoleon the Small, the Double Charlatan, the Devil's Favourite, Bonaparte the Brigand Chief.[37] If only through repetition, some of these smears must have rubbed off on the British public.

6

Re-burial and Reconciliation

Attempts to have Napoleon's remains transferred from St Helena to Paris, as he would have wished, began within a few months of his death. Bertrand and Montholon were in London by 1821, and as well as delivering their package to Holland House for Lady Holland (see p. 107), they addressed a letter to George IV (who had succeeded his father as King in the previous year). In this, transmitted through Liverpool, the Prime Minister, they said that they claimed the dead man's ashes.* 'Your ministers, Sire,' they wrote, 'know that it was his desire to lie among the people he loved so much.' There followed a thrust about Hudson Lowe refusing to grant this wish, and the name of Madame Mère, Napoleon's mother, was invoked: 'she begs you to return her son's ashes to her, she asks for the slight consolation of watering his tomb with her tears.' As the old lady was living in Rome, and would certainly have been refused entry into Bourbon-controlled France, even for the purpose of tomb-watering, this pathos-laden plea must be

*Napoleon's remains did not, of course, consist of ashes. His body, less the heart and entrails, remained entire and, as the exhumation was later to show, was in a remarkable state of preservation (see p. 150). But the whole process of bringing the corpse to Paris is habitually described in French as 'le Retour des Cendres'.

read as a piece of French rhetoric, on a par with Napoleon's comparison of Themistocles with himself, which had made Croker laugh so much.

The former Emperor's body was obviously no laughing matter, but all the same the eloquence of the Frenchmen fell on deaf ears. It was not until December of that year that the British Ambassador in Paris was instructed to make it known that his government would relinquish 'the ashes' as soon as the French government 'signified their desire for them'. There was no sign that this was about to happen. Nor did a direct approach from Madame Mère herself to Lord Castlereagh have any more effect. She wrote on 15 August 1821, Napoleon's birthday:

> the mother of the Emperor Napoleon comes to plead that his enemies will return her son's ashes . . . what pretext can be found for refusing to give up those immortal remains? . . . I implore His Britannic Majesty to grant me my son's remains. I gave Napoleon to France and to the world. In the name of God, in the name of all mothers, I come before you as a suppliant, my Lord . . .

There seems to have been no reply, and no mention of Madame Mère's approach appears in the twelve volumes of Castlereagh's dispatches and correspondence.

The years passed. Napoleon slept on under the willow trees, and his legend, supported and diffused by Victor Hugo, Stendhal and Béranger, took hold and spread through many layers of French society. Forgetful of the human sacrifices demanded of them by the unbridled ambitions of the Emperor, French people, or at least a sizeable portion of them, wallowed in a bottomless pool of nostalgia and longing for a return to the epoch of Imperial glory. In 1830 the Bourbon dynasty as a ruling house came to an end when the unpopular and absolutist Charles X was overthrown and succeeded by Louis-Philippe, of the Orléans side of the family, who was not proclaimed King of France but King of the French. But Bonapartism was still a force to be reckoned with: Napoleon's son, the so-called King of Rome, Duke of Reichstadt, by now aged twenty, was alive and (fairly) well in Vienna and had his supporters in France. In England, the curiosity factor which had characterised British attitudes towards the defeated Emperor found new expression when his stepdaughter and sister-in-law Hortense, ex-Queen of Holland and mother of the future Napoleon III, came to London with her son in 1831 and did the social rounds. Three years earlier, the author and traveller the Marquis de Custine had noted that in London Napoleon I had become a 'hero of melodrama and pantomime'.[†]

Louis-Philippe's reign became increasingly beset with unrest and popular protest. He had tried to contain Bonapartism by such gestures as attending in 1833 the inauguration of Napoleon's statue on the column in the Place Vendôme, when he doffed his plumed hat and cried, 'Long live the Emperor!' The pressure was somewhat relieved by the death in June 1832 of the Duke of Reichstadt and the ignominious failure by Louis Napoleon, the Emperor's nephew and future Napoleon III, to raise the flag of revolt at Strasbourg in 1836. But despite these developments, the internal situation remained precarious; in 1839 and 1840 strikes affected the whole country. Something needed to be done to stem the rising tide of discontent, and Adolphe Thiers, the Prime Minister and author of a massive history of the French Revolution, had a suggestion. Louis-Philippe took a lot of persuading that the return of Napoleon's remains was a good idea, but in the end he conceded and told Thiers, in May 1840, to go ahead and seek the British government's agreement.

[†]Chateaubriand, who was French Ambassador in London after the Bourbon restoration, wrote that in 1822 'I found this great city steeped in Bonapartist memories; from disparagement people had swung to a foolish enthusiasm. Memoirs of Bonaparte were everywhere; his bust adorned every chimney-piece ...' (*Mémoires d'Outre-Tombe*, Paris, Dufort, Mulet et Boulanger, 1860, vol. IV, pp. 244–5.

Everything now moved with remarkable speed. Thiers told the British Ambassador in Paris, Lord Granville,[1] that 'nothing would more tend to cement the union between the two nations and create a friendly feeling towards England in France than the acquiescence of the British government' to the return of the late Emperor's body. Another French historian, Guizot, serving as Louis-Philippe's Ambassador in London, was instructed on 4 May to seek British consent. 'I do not know,' Thiers wrote to Guizot, 'any honourable motive for refusal . . . England cannot tell the world that she wishes to keep a corpse prisoner.' The Ambassador was inclined at first to be sceptical; 'was it for King Louis-Philippe' he wondered in his memoirs[2] 'to glorify and bring back to life a rival? . . . to anyone of common-sense crowds of objections present themselves'. But he added that 'there is generosity and majesty in the project'. He addressed a note to Palmerston, the Foreign Secretary, conveying the request and expressing the certainty that the British government 'will see nothing in this desire of His Majesty the King of the French but just and pious feelings'. The Cabinet in London saw no objection, and nor did the Duke of Wellington, who was Leader of the Opposition (his response was typical: he said that the French would be sure to make it a matter of triumph over England, but that personally 'he did not care one two-penny damn about that').[3] Granville was instructed to inform Thiers of the decision, together with the hope that 'the readiness with which this answer is given will be looked upon in France as proof of the desire of Her Majesty's Government to obliterate every remnant of these national animosities which, during the life of the Emperor, assayed the French and English peoples in arms against each other', and which 'will be buried in the grave to which these remains are about to be consigned'. This cross-channel exchange of elevated sentiments and (premature) anticipation of the *Entente Cordiale* of sixty years later was not quite all it seemed, at least on the British side. The government in London was anxious that the business of fetching Napoleon's body from St Helena should be as inconspicuously conducted as possible 'and especially', as Palmerston wrote to Granville on 16 May, 'without any allusion or reference to the former situation of Napoleon Bonaparte as a prisoner at St Helena, in order to avoid anything that might possibly give rise to feelings of irritation in the minds of the British public'.

Was this a tacit admission, a quarter of a century after the event, that the treatment of Napoleon at St Helena was nothing to be proud of? Or, on the other hand, did the government suspect that public opinion might feel 'irritation' at the idea of the 'Corsican ogre' having his own funerary wishes finally granted? In any event, Thiers gave assurances that all would be seemly – no speeches, no demonstrations; painters and writers liable to cause trouble (Victor Hugo springs to mind) would be kept away. One British concession had to be made, on Thiers' insistence: throughout the procedure and in any report to be made, the title of 'Emperor' should be used; the demeaning appellation of General Bonaparte was something that could not be tolerated by France.

So the expedition set out to bring Napoleon home. It was led, at least in name, by the Prince de Joinville, the twenty-two-year-old third son of Louis-Philippe. The effective head of the delegation was a young diplomat of the Rohan-Chabot family, the Comte de Jarnac. He had served in the French Embassy in London and had been chosen, Thiers explained, precisely because he was not connected in any way with the years of captivity at St Helena. The four comrades of that unhappy time who sailed in the frigate *La Belle Poule* in July 1840 were Bertrand, the former Grand Marshal, who took with him his son Arthur, born on the island in 1817 (he was the baby presented to Napoleon by Mme. Bertrand as 'the first Frenchman who has entered the island without Hudson Lowe's permission'); Emmanuel Las Cases, the son of Las Cases, who was not well enough to go; Gourgaud, and Marchand the chief valet. There were as well half a dozen of the Longwood servants. They were all instructed to remain silent and impassive at the exhumation

149

and other proceedings; as Thiers wrote to Guizot in London, 'the English Cabinet will have no reason to regret its decision'.

The voyage took nearly three months. Once arrived at St Helena, the reception by the British authorities was all that could be desired, even by the most prickly Frenchman. The Governor, Major-General Middlemore, was unwell, but he sent his son, an army captain, to greet the French frigate. Royal Naval ships and shore batteries fired a salute of twenty-one guns and *La Belle Poule* responded in kind. Joinville, accompanied by Jarnac and others, went to Plantation House to pay their respects to the ailing Governor with whom, two days later, they all dined. On 15 October, twenty-five years to the day since Napoleon first arrived at St Helena, the task of exhuming the body began. Joinville had wanted the whole thing to be managed by his sailors, but the Governor insisted that arrangements should be left in British hands. Local workmen and British soldiers worked throughout the night in pouring rain to raise the coffin, and it was not until the following morning that twelve bare-headed soldiers carried Napoleon's remains, in their quadruple coffins, into a specially erected tent.

At this point, General Middlemore arrived and was there to witness the opening of the last coffin and the exposure of Napoleon's body. Guillard, the doctor from *La Belle Poule*, slowly rolled back the satin covering, which had been laid over the corpse nineteen years before, to reveal the astonishingly lifelike and well preserved features of the dead man. The on-lookers, deeply moved, had only two minutes to gaze on what lay before them before Jarnac ordered the coffins to be resealed. The tin, mahogany and lead casings of 1821 were placed inside the sarcophagus brought from France in the frigate, so that Napoleon now lay within six coffins. Captain Alexander, commanding the army engineers, handed the gilt key of the sarcophagus to Jarnac, and then the enormous load, weighing 1,200 kilogrammes, was borne by 43 British soldiers to the hearse waiting on the track above. Reaching the main road, it began its journey to Jamestown, the capital, accompanied by three companies of the 91st Regiment, a detachment of the local militia, with band, and followed by the party of French mourners. Middlemore, despite his illness, marched the six kilometres, and having arrived at the quayside announced to the waiting Joinville that in the name of the British government he was handing over the coffin. Accompanied by salvos from the shore batteries, it was then placed on a launch and rowed by French sailors to the *La Belle Poule*. The next day, Joinville wanted to sail immediately, but there were still formalities to be completed, including the preparation of the official report and the distribution of French medals for all those on the island who had played any part in the proceedings. Finally, on the morning of 18 October 1840, the frigate and her naval escorts weighed anchor, and their precious cargo began the long voyage home. The British connection with the first Napoleon had, it seemed, drawn to a dignified conclusion. Or, as Martineau sourly puts it: 'England, as if embarrassed by her memories, had given to the dead the honours she had grudged to the living.'

But the historical conflict between the British and Napoleon, or at least his body, was to undergo one last phase. While *La Belle Poule* was making her way northwards, French and British policy over Egypt was diverging to a point where, instead of new-found amity between the two nations, war seemed once more a possibility. The trouble involved the Albanian adventurer, Mehemet Ali, who had earlier established his authority over Egypt and challenged the integrity of the Ottoman Empire. France, who through Napoleon's conquest in 1798 had staked out an interest in Egypt, supported Mehemet Ali. This brought her, by 1840, to a collision course with Britain who, under Palmerston's vigorous handling, entered into an alliance with Austria, Prussia and Russia with the purpose of containing Mehemet Ali. The latter, after a British naval force had captured Beirut and Acre, had to evacuate Asia Minor and Syria. In Paris, Thiers declared that good relations with London were shattered and the French press uttered fierce threats. The affair took on the likeness of a rehearsal for the Fashoda crisis, the episode in 1898 involving an insignificant place on the Upper Nile where rival French and British claims brought the two countries close to war.

But King Louis-Philippe had no intention of going to war with England, and before long the tension subsided. Of all this, Joinville and his staff had no idea as the *La Belle Poule* sailed along. It was not until, in November, the frigate caught up with a Dutch schooner that they learned from her captain that fighting had broken out in the Mediterranean and that France and the four great powers were at loggerheads. Was it possible, was it conceivable, that if *La Belle Poule* met a British man-of-war, Napoleon might become once more a British prisoner? Joinville seemed to have thought so, because he ordered the frigate to be made ready for hostilities. The elegant furnishings of the cabins were flung into the sea, the temporary partitions demolished, the guns made ready. Orders were given that if the worst came to the worst and capture was imminent, it would be better for the ship to be sunk and for the Emperor's body to finish up in a watery grave than for it to pass into the hands of his former enemy.*

But the worst did not come. Nothing came, except the onward progress of the frigate, which finally arrived, intact, at Cherbourg on 30 November, whence the coffin was conveyed to Le Havre and the mouth of the Seine. From there it was carried by water to Paris where, on 15 December, it was received by the King at the Invalides with due pomp and ceremony, though another twenty years were to elapse before it found its final resting place under the great gilded dome.

An English witness to these ceremonies was William Makepeace Thackeray. He spent the autumn of 1840 in Paris, where he temporarily put his poor demented wife into a *maison de santé*.

---

*See Martineau, *Le Retour des Cendres,* Paris 1990 Tallandier, p. 124.

He described what he had seen (or imagined) to Miss Smith, a notional young English friend in London, and these lively and often satirical reports were published in January 1841, with the title of 'The Second Funeral of Napoleon'. Thackeray was no Bonapartist. He had previously composed a highly critical essay on 'Napoleon and his system', which was published in July 1840 in *The Paris Sketch Book*. The essay is an answer to a pamphlet by Louis Napoleon, the future Emperor, extolling the merits of his uncle. Thackeray recalls that twenty-five-years earlier 'we used to call Napoleon the bloody Corsican upstart and assassin' and describes his system as 'a military despotism'. The first Emperor was, admits Thackeray, a fine administrator, legislator and constructor of public works, but while all this was accomplished without new loans or exorbitant taxes 'it was only the blood and liberty of the people that were taxed'.

Thackeray's presence at Napoleon's funeral was not his first connection with the Emperor. At the age of six, accompanied by his cousin, Richard Shakespear, and in the charge of an Indian servant, he was sent home from India, where his father, who died in 1815, had been in the service of the East India Company. The ship on which the party travelled put in, as most west-bound ships did, at St Helena, where 'my black servant took me a long walk over rocks and hills until we reached a garden, where we saw a man walking . . . "that is he" said the black servant, "that is Bonaparte, he eats three sheep every day, and all the little children he can lay hands on"'.‡⁴

‡This picture of Bonaparte eating children is a recurrent one during the Napoleonic Wars; could it have been the work of some early version of a black propaganda department in London? John Julius Norwich has drawn my attention to the following nineteenth-century lullaby:

Baby, baby, naughty baby,	Baby, baby, if he hears you
Hush, you squalling thing,	As he gallops past the house,
I say, peace this moment, peace or maybe	Limb from limb at once he'll tear you,
Bonaparte will pass this way.	Just as pussy tears a mouse.

His account of the funeral is a fine piece of Thackeray's early writing (though it was not a publishing success). It is full of satire, irony and fun-poking at what he considered to be the pretentious and tawdry ceremonial. For Thackeray, like Carlyle in his 1840 lectures on heroes and hero-worship, saw Napoleon as a charlatan and quack. But here he is mocking the funeral and not the corpse. He told Miss Smith: 'They say that on the passage of Napoleon's coffin down the Seine, old soldiers and country people walked miles from their villages just to catch a sight of the boat which carried his body . . . God forbid that we should quarrel with such prayers and sorrow . . . something great and good must have been in this man' – a sentiment that is probably as close to the feelings of the average Briton as any amount of research is likely to get.

Though some of his descriptions are imaginary, Thackeray, under his pen-name of Michael Angelo Titmarsh, was present in the church of the Invalides when Napoleon's remains were borne in. He had plenty of time to observe the scene, having arrived at 9 a.m. to wait at least five hours until the arrival of the procession. His description is the reverse of flattering. He makes fun of the Archbishop of Paris's mitre – 'formed within probably of consecrated cardboard' – he mocks the 'weak, snuffling lugubrious manner' of the chanting, and even the sight of the coffin, when it finally appears, fails to impress him – 'a box covered with a great red cross, a dingy-looking crown on the top of it'.

Although he liked Paris and had many French friends, Thackeray took a pessimistic view of Anglo-French relations. This was founded not so much on his anti-Napoleonic views as on his reading of history. For eight hundred years, he tells his

---

Baby, baby, he's a giant,
Tall and black as Monmouth steeple,
And he breakfasts, dines and suppers
Every day on naughty people.

And he'll beat you, beat you, beat you,
And he'll beat you all to pap,
And he'll eat you, eat you, eat you,
Every morsel, snap, snap, snap.

imaginary English friend, 'the French hate us . . . men get a
character for patriotism in France merely by hating England'. It
is a long story, he goes on, and the hatred 'has been transmitted
on the French side from father to son'. The feeling is not, he
claims, reciprocal, and that is because Britain 'has had no, or
few, defeats, no invasions to make us angry'. That thought leads
him on to mock the Prince de Joinville's fears, as *La Belle Poule*
sailed northwards, of a clash with Royal Naval ships and his
action in throwing the furniture overboard.

Thackeray was an individualist, full of irony and a sense of the
ridiculous. He was also an inexhaustibly prolific writer, who
could and did rattle on, page after page, on almost any topic.
His jaundiced analysis of the relationship between Britain and
France need not be taken too seriously, though his dislike and
distrust of flowery French expressions is to this day probably
shared by many of his compatriots. What is much more
remarkable than Thackeray's mocking is the rapidity with which
British animosities towards Napoleon (not felt, of course, by the
Holland House set and those who agreed with them) died away
or were transformed into a measure of admiration. It was as
though the Emperor's reinterment in the Invalides closed an
epic chapter in British and European history . . . as indeed it
did.

No one realised or expressed this better than the young
Queen Victoria. It took the force of circumstance to persuade
her to look with increasing favour on the Bonapartist dynasty.
In 1848 Louis-Philippe, faced with popular revolt, had had to
abdicate and flee the country. With Queen Amélie he arrived in
England, like so many other French royal or Bonapartist exiles,
past and future. Queen Victoria showed great pity and solici-
tude, her feelings reinforced by family ties; her beloved Uncle
Leopold was married to the daughter of the French King.
When subsequently Louis Napoleon, by then Emperor, con-
fiscated the Orléans estates in France, no one was more indignant than Victoria and Albert; 'the violent seizure of the

poor Orléans' property,' wrote the latter, 'is a crime that cries to heaven'.[5] The Queen's letters and diaries are full of expressions of sympathy for the dispossessed Orléans family. As for Napoleon III, who had consolidated his leadership in France by means of a blood-soaked coup d'état in December 1852, the Queen was outraged by the approval of the new regime expressed by Lord Palmerston, the Foreign Secretary, to the French Ambassador in London, without any prior consultation. Admittedly, her ire had more to do with Palmerston's conduct than with her feelings about the Bonapartist adventurer. But her attitude towards him was, at least initially, equivocal where it was not downright disapproving. She was genuinely shocked by the application of the newly proclaimed Emperor to be allowed to marry her niece, Princess Adelaide, the daughter of Princess Feodora, the Queen's half-sister. When the seventeen-year-old Princess turned down the proposal, Victoria wrote to her half-sister: 'I feel that your dear child is saved from ruin of every possible sort . . . you know what he [Louis Napoleon] is, what his moral behaviour is . . .' The Prince Consort was even more censorious. To the end of his short life, he veered between cautious acceptance of the new Emperor and deeply felt dislike and fear. In 1859, after Britain and France had been allied for several years, he wrote that he, Louis Napoleon, 'has been born and bred a conspirator and at his present age will never get out of this turn of mind'.

The Queen, with her habitual shrewdness, was more circumspect. Though she thought Louis Napoleon 'such an extraordinary man, one can never be for one instant safe', and she counselled caution as he prepared to assume the Imperial title; 'objectionable as this appellation no doubt is [was this a conscious or perhaps subconscious reference to the original "Corsican upstart"?], it may hardly be worth offending France and her Ruler by refusing to recognise it . . . our object should be to leave France alone, as long as she is not aggressive'.

A little more than two years later, the outbreak of the Crimean War brought Britain and France together in a military alliance. However mistrustful British opinion remained of Bonapartist aims and ambitions, whether harboured by the first or the third Emperor, *realpolitik* was *real*, and so in the spring of 1854 the wary Prince Albert visited Boulogne to witness French military manoeuvres and hold conversations with Napoleon III. *Punch* celebrated the occasions with a quizzical poem:

> I wonder what his thoughts were, that sad-eyed, silent man,
> As alongside Boulogne's jetty England's royal steamer ran,
> While with a King beside him[§] that adventurer was seen
> Greeting, as Emperor of France, the Consort of our Queen?

The meeting between Emperor and Prince passed off amicably enough. But Queen Victoria, a woman of pronounced sensibilities, was to react much more warmly to the imperial charm which Napoleon deployed when in the Queen's presence, with unremitting zeal – it served his interests to do so. In April 1855 he and his recently married Empress were the Queen's guests at Windsor (where the Waterloo chamber was tactfully, if temporarily, renamed the Music Room).[#] Prince Albert, in a rare flash of humour, thought that precautions should be taken to prevent George III from turning in his grave in the crypt of St George's chapel.[6] The Queen was much more positive, writing

---

[§]King Leopold of the Belgians was also the guest of the Emperor.

[#]This renaming, however short-lived, caused some alarm when it became known about in Berlin. Prince Albert drafted a letter for the Queen to send to the Princess of Prussia, in which she explained that 'as for the Waterloo Room, it has kept its name, but so that it should not constantly ring in the ears of our guest, when there was a concert in the room, it was called the Music Room on the programme' (Royal Archives, VIC/Y 128/23-4 22 May 1855).

to Uncle Leopold: 'I am much pleased with our Imperial guests, who behave really with the greatest tact.'[7] By this time Queen and Emperor were addressing one another, according to the protocol for correspondence between reigning sovereigns, as brother and sister – '*Bonne Soeur*' and '*Mon Cher Frère*' – a development about which the Prince Consort wrote to his brother[8] that 'the *Mon Frère* must not become *frère* Cain'. (The Tsar of Russia was having none of all this and persisted in addressing the French Emperor as '*Mon cher Ami*'.)

There was no sign of Cain-like tendencies at Windsor in the spring of 1855. After the visit, the Queen wrote a long and acutely observant analysis of Napoleon III's character and motives, in which critical objectivity is mixed with personal admiration. She clearly had fallen under his spell, writing of his 'power of fascination, the effect of which upon all those who become more intimately acquainted with him [e.g. herself] is *most sensibly* felt'. She could hardly not be conscious of the contrast between Anglo-French relations in 1855 and the not-far-distant past, writing of 'the very intimate alliance which now unites England and France, for so many centuries the bitterest enemies and rivals, and this, under the reign of the present Emperor, the nephew of our greatest foe and bearing his name . . .' She had already recorded in her journal (17 April 1855) her feelings about 'George III's granddaughter [dancing] with the nephew of our great enemy, the Emperor Napoleon, now my most firm Ally, in the Waterloo Gallery . . . incredible'. This is not the only reference in her reflections about Napoleon III to her grandfather's bitter hostility to the first Napoleon. Perhaps she was acquainted with what George III had said, with his habitual reiteration, in 1803: 'I should like to fight Boney single-handed . . . I am sure I should. I should give him a hiding, I'm sure I should, I'm sure of it.'[9]

What the Queen found striking in the person she again called 'this most extraordinary man' was the 'wonderful tact in his conduct and manners . . . in which many a King's son, nurtured in palaces and educated in the midst of affairs, never succeeded in attaining'. As though to show that she was not completely star-struck, however, she observed that the Emperor would not 'hesitate to do a thing by main force, even if in itself unjust and tyrannical, should he consider that the accomplishment of his destiny demanded it'.

A few months later in that hot summer of 1855, the Queen and Prince Consort, accompanied by the Prince of Wales and the Princess Royal, paid a state visit to Paris, the first British sovereign to do so since Henry VI had been crowned King of France in Notre-Dame in 1431. It was a splendid occasion, the Emperor going to great lengths to please and entertain his guests. The Queen became almost ecstatic about her reception and especially about Louis Napoleon's attentions to her. She wrote to Baron Stockmar,[10] friend and adviser to Albert and herself:

> For the Emperor personally I conceived a real affection and friendship . . . I cannot say how pleasant and easy it is to live with him or how attached one becomes to him . . . he is so simple and unaffected, never making *des phrases* or making compliments [surely a mistaken judgement] . . . he has the power of attaching those to him who come near to him and know him, which is *quite incredible*'.

It is impossible to resist the thought that the Queen, who was only thirty-four and highly-sexed, momentarily fell half, or perhaps more than half, in love with the flattering Frenchman. She was sufficiently honest, however, to admit, in her letter to Stockmar, that Albert was 'less enthusiastic than I am'.

One of the high points of the visit, and one which dramatically illustrates the change that had come about in British feelings towards the first Napoleon, was the royal homage paid to the latter's remains in the Invalides. As before at Windsor, the Queen could not get out of her mind the comparison, in terms of relations between the two countries, of the present with the past. 'There I stood,' she tells her journal, 'at the arm of Napoleon III, his nephew, before the coffin of England's bitterest foe; for I, the granddaughter of that King who hated him most, and who most vigorously opposed him, being my nearest and dearest ally.'

The great well-like vault which today surrounds the vast sarcophagus containing Bonaparte's bones was not complete in 1855, though the Queen and the Emperor leaned on the marble balustrade and looked down into the empty space. (The Emperor remarked that it looked like a pool, the sheen of the polished marble giving it the appearance of water.) Then they moved to the nearby chapel of St Jérome, where the coffin lay, covered with a bee-embroidered velvet pall; at the foot were the hat worn by Napoleon at Eylau and the sword he had carried at Austerlitz. General Canrobert, formerly the commander of the French forces in the Crimea, gives in his memoirs a vivid eye-witness description of the scene:

> Everyone contemplated the coffin in silence . . . after a moment of meditation, of absolute silence, the Queen, with a respectful, calm and severe expression, turned to the [thirteen-year-old] Prince of Wales, and putting her hand on his shoulder said "Kneel down before the tomb of the great Napoleon". At that moment, a terrible storm, to which the torrid heat of the last few days had been working up, burst forth. Great peals of thunder shook all the windows of the chapel, and their sound went echoing round the vault. Rapid and ceaseless flashes of lightning gave an almost supernatural aspect to the moving and solemn scene, by continually illuminating it with an unnatural brilliance . . . Waterloo, St Helena, the English alliance, England in the person of her Queen and of the future King who was kneeling before the remains of Napoleon; all that made my senses reel . . . I could no longer control myself and began to weep'.[11]

The Times correspondent passes over this historic moment in a few lines – probably he did not witness it – but also records the storm and the rain, commenting, 'well might nature show signs of elemental agitation while such an act of homage to the ashes of the mighty dead was in progress'.

The Queen herself, though remaining dry-eyed, was also moved by what she described in her journal as 'this solemn scene', 'this strange and wonderful tribute of respect to a departed foe', setting the 'seal of Heaven' on the unity between two great and powerful nations. Such rapturous thoughts were, no doubt, the natural result of a uniquely moving experience. The Queen's vision of lasting friendship and understanding between Britain and France was destined to be shattered time and time again in the years to come. But at the least it places the Queen in the interesting stance of a latter-day Napoleonist, ready to forgive if not forget the human and material sacrifices imposed so recently on Britain by the Napoleonic Wars under their inspired and implacable protagonist.

Only forty years had passed since the defeated Emperor wrote the Themistocles letter to the Prince Regent, invoking British hospitality, a letter which received no reply. Were it possible to experience posthumous sensations, the restless spirit whose coffin lies within the Invalides 'by the banks of the Seine' would surely have felt a degree of satisfaction at the sight of the future Edward VII, himself a contributor to the *Entente Cordiale* of the next century, kneeling reverently before his earthly remains.

APPENDIX I

What Happened to Sir Hudson Lowe

The account has already been given in Chapter 3 of George IV's enthusiastic reception of Lowe on his return from St Helena in the autumn of 1821: 'I congratulate you most sincerely, etc.' Lowe, despite his awareness of the accusations being made against him by Napoleonists of various kinds,* would have been less than human if he had not been encouraged by his sovereign's words to think that further prizes might come his way. He was only fifty-two and had performed, and been praised for performing, an unpleasant and arduous task; also, he was not well off. The only immediate reward, however, was the colonelcy of a regiment – the 93rd – certainly an honour but hardly an adequate one for six years of the kind of trials that Lowe had had to undergo.

There the process of preferment seemed to falter. Worse still, the aggrieved O'Meara was on the warpath. Already in 1819 he had fired his first shot with the publication of a pamphlet with the title 'An exposition of some of the Transactions that have

---

*The attacks took a violent form when the young Emmanual Las Cases, Las Cases' son, assaulted Lowe in a London street and challenged him to a duel. Lowe disregarded the challenge (Forsyth, vol. III, p. 316).

taken place at St Helena since the appointment of Sir Hudson Lowe as Governor of that Island'. Taking it under notice, the *Edinburgh Review* sided with O'Meara, arguing that the conditions of captivity should be alleviated before it was too late. Emboldened, O'Meara set to work to expand this relatively modest contribution into 'A Voice from St Helena', published in 1822. Dedicated to Lady Holland, the work is in the form of a diary, recounting O'Meara's numerous conversations with Napoleon and also his increasingly bruising encounters with Lowe. His accounts of the latter are full of descriptions of the Governor being in 'a paroxysm of rage', in 'a violent passion', uttering 'furious exclamations' and invective. O'Meara depicts himself, on the other hand, as remaining calm and dignified, although he is vigorous in his refusal to be a spy or informer about what was happening at Longwood.

Opinions about the worth of O'Meara's book differ. It certainly caused a sensation and was a publishing success, being translated into several languages. This is not surprising, whatever the value of the testimony. As the only British citizen ever to have known Napoleon really well and to have had close contact with him almost daily over a period of three years, he was uniquely placed to arouse the curiosity of the public. The usually crusty Carlyle thought well of the 'Voice': 'O'Meara's work has increased my respect for Napoleon.' Walter Scott, on the other hand, described it as the output of a disappointed man.[1] Moreover, he detected that the most spiteful passages about Lowe were inserted later, 'under the influence of recollection, sharpened by any passion'. At a later date, Rosebery (see Appendix II) considered 'O'Meara's evidence worthless and obviously tainted'. At a later date still, M. Gilbert Martineau, the guardian of the shrine at St Helena and chief castigator of Lowe, wrote that O'Meara's testimony was 'sometimes mocking, sometimes sarcastic, but always implacable . . . Sir Hudson Lowe was branded for ever as infamous by one of his own staff [untrue: O'Meara was attached to Longwood and not on the Governor's staff], and his portrait hung in the rogues' gallery of history'.[2]

Lowe at once realised and felt the effect of the 'Voice'. In a memorandum addressed to the Prime Minister, Lord Liverpool, he wrote of 'the cravings of the most credulous, the most inquisitive, or the most malignant mind' and added bitterly that 'I was destined to be the real victim, upon whom the public indignation was to fall'.[3] He decided to take legal action. In August 1822 he consulted the Solicitor-General, Sir John Copley (later Lord Lyndhurst), and the Chief Justice of the Court of Common Pleas, Tindal. They advised him to draw up a schedule of what he considered to be the most objectionable and libellous of O'Meara's allegations, with a view to bringing a case of criminal libel. This was no easy task. As Lowe complained, O'Meara had written his book in such a way that it was very difficult to disentangle truth from falsehood, to reveal 'the meshes of the plot which had thus been so artificially woven to accomplish the ruin of my public and private character'.[4]

By the time Lowe had assembled his material, eight months had passed since the publication of the offending volumes. Although the court presided over by the Lord Chief Justice (Abbott, later Lord Tenterden) granted leave to proceed with the case, he drew attention to what he called the lateness of the application. Lowe busied himself obtaining twenty-one affidavits, including testimony from Sir Thomas Reade, Sir George Bingham, many officers from the regiments stationed at St Helena during the period, Balcombe the purveyor, and many others. O'Meara, for his part, assembled seventeen affidavits, including those from other regimental officers, among them Major Poppleton, one of the orderly officers at Longwood, and statements from Montholon, Las Cases, Dr Antommacchi and some of the Longwood servants. But nothing of this evidence was ever called. When the case came on, O'Meara's counsel went straight to the lateness point, with the result that the case was dismissed and Lowe left to pay his own costs.

How did this fiasco come about? Lowe claimed that his papers – presumably the list of O'Meara's alleged libels – were with the Solicitor-General for nearly four months. If this were true, it would seem that he was the victim of legal sluggishness, as prevalent in the 1820s as it is today. But it is hard to avoid the conclusion that Lowe, a man of wide and varied administrative experience, failed to act in the matter with all the force and application which his own interests demanded. Once the legal case had fallen apart, there was nothing to stop him from issuing, in public form, a detailed refutation of O'Meara's smears. This is exactly what Bathurst, to whom Lowe appealed, advised him to do: 'you owe it to yourself,' he wrote in November 1823, 'to draw up a full and complete vindication of the administration of your government at St Helena, coupled with all the documents in your statement.' Yet Lowe did nothing. It was indeed rather late to do anything effective. He appears to have been so convinced of the rectitude of his attitude towards, and actions concerning, Napoleon as to think it would be beneath his dignity to enter into a public argument with O'Meara. That, at least, is the explanation offered by Forsyth, his main protagonist,[5] but it is irreconcilable with Lowe's original wish to take O'Meara to law. Perhaps he felt discouraged by the government's attitude in general. If so, he had reason. Bathurst, who seems to have been sympathetic towards his cause, had recommended him for a pension, but no pension was ever forthcoming, although his predecessor as Governor of St Helena, Colonel Wilks, was granted a generous one.

Bathurst did, it is true, hold out the hope of another post, this time a West Indian governorship, and was as good as his word. In December 1823 Lowe was offered the governorship of Antigua. He declined it, for family reasons, and after two years of enforced idleness he was appointed GOC of the forces in Ceylon. The Lowes left England in October 1825, travelling overland as far as Constantinople.

Lowe was still in Ceylon when Sir Walter Scott's massive biography of Napoleon was published in 1828. He had been hoping that at last he would be vindicated by the judgement of a great writer, who moreover had had access to some of the official papers relating to Napoleon's captivity. His hopes were disappointed, or so he considered. Scott did not provide the clean bill he had expected. In particular, he suggested, as O'Meara had done, that as Napoleon's custodian, Lowe let his temper get the better of him. The fallen Emperor, Scott claimed, should not have been made 'subject like other men to retort and retaliation'. Read today, the criticism does not seem especially sharp. Scott speaks of 'traces of a warm and irritable temper which seems sometimes to have overborne his [Lowe's] discretion'. Even when Napoleon was being 'most unreasonable and most provoking', Lowe ought to have remained 'cool and unruffled'.

Lowe's chagrin is easy to understand. His own records and the independent witness of Admiral Malcolm leave little or no doubt that, though sorely provoked by Bonaparte's insulting outbursts, he commendably kept his temper and resisted the temptation to reply in kind. Forsyth[6] says that Scott, though he had access to Colonial Office sources, had not seen Lowe's own papers. The point underlines Lowe's folly in not preparing and publishing his own refutation of O'Meara.

Disappointed and hurt – 'for it was not an enemy that reproached him, then he could have borne it'[7] – he sought and obtained leave to go to England to see what could be done in his interests. His sea passage, like most of those from the East, took him to St Helena, where he was fêted and given a heart-warming welcome. He went to Longwood, vacated only seven years before, to find it in a state of total disrepair; Napoleon's death chamber had become a stable and the servants' quarters a pigsty. Arrived in London, his welcome was not so encouraging. Bathurst, by this time Lord President of the Council in a government of which Wellington was Prime Minister, was, as usual, friendly, assuring Lowe that the government had not changed its mind about his St Helena record and that there was no need to reply to Scott. The best thing that he, Lowe, could do, if he wanted to succeed to the governorship of Ceylon, would be to return there without delay, so as to be on the spot when the vacancy occurred.

Lowe's subsequent meeting with the Prime Minister was still more discouraging. Wellington refused to make any commitment about the governorship of Ceylon and was equally negative about the prospects of a pension. He did, however, say, for what it was worth, that he thought Lowe had 'been very hardly used'.

Lowe returned to his post in Ceylon, as advised by Bathurst, but the governorship went to someone else, and by 1831 he was back in England. He never got another public post. In 1843, a year before his death at the age of seventy-four, he drew up yet another memorandum, pointing out that in the previous twelve years, the governorship of Ceylon had three times fallen vacant and the post of High Commissioner in Corfu and the Ionian Islands (where he had distinguished himself thirty years earlier) had changed hands four times, 'but on none of these occasions were either my local or general services, or any other claim arising from past disappointments taken into consideration, which I should have hoped might have been their due'.

There are only two consoling elements in this sad story. The first is represented by the action, after Lowe's death, of Sir Robert Peel, as Prime Minister, in arranging the grant of a small pension to Lowe's unmarried daughter 'in recognition of the services of her father'. The second concerned the role of the Duke of Wellington, who had such an unfavourable view of Lowe as Napoleon's custodian.

On 19 February 1833, in a debate in the House of Lords about a coercion bill for Ireland, Lord Teynham, discussing the extent of the powers to be granted to the Lord-Lieutenant, hypothesised on the possibility of the then holder of that office, Lord Normanby, being succeeded 'by a Sir Hudson Lowe'. Wellington rose to defend 'the character of a highly respectable officer, not a member of this House, from a gross imputation thrown upon him (by implication) by the noble Lord; and certainly a grosser one I never heard uttered within these walls . . . I have the honour to know Sir Hudson Lowe, and I will say, in this House or elsewhere, wherever it may be, that there is not in the army a more respectable officer than Sir Hudson Lowe, nor has His Majesty a more faithful subject'.

Teynham denied that he had cast aspersions on Lowe, and then, in the next breath, did precisely that, saying that 'as regards his conduct while Governor of St Helena, I say, and will maintain it as a peer of Parliament, that he is cried out upon by all the people of Europe as a person not to be trusted with power'. Bathurst now entered the fray: 'Sir Hudson Lowe behaved, in his very responsible capacity, in a manner highly to his credit; all well-informed persons in Europe knew what his conduct was, and approved it.' Two days later, Teynham made another, and this time genuine, apology to 'the gallant General'.

A grateful Lowe wrote to Wellington, thanking him for what he had said, and Wellington, always punctilious with correspondence, replied that 'I did no more than my duty . . . in repelling a very gross and marked insinuation against an officer, in his absence, for whom I entertained the highest respect and regard'. As on so many other occasions, Wellington's sense of fairness and loyalty overcame all other considerations – even though he had once described Lowe as 'a damned fool' – so that one of the most maligned public servants in recent history finally achieved some portion of the vindication which he had sought for so long.

Appendix II

Hardy and Rosebery:
Two Approaches to Napoleon

It would be the work and effort of a lifetime to summarise, let alone dissect, the books in English about Napoleon (in the computerised catalogue in the Bibliothèque Nationale in Paris, it is said that if you enter 'Napoleon' and press the button, you would have to sit there for forty-eight hours for all the titles to come up on the screen). To this day, he remains one of the if not *the* most written-about characters in history; in the index to that monumental example of compression, H.A.L. Fisher's *History of Europe*, Napoleon has a longer entry than any other single person.

Despite the immense choice, two English writers in particular seem worthy of individual comment: Thomas Hardy and Lord Rosebery.* The first because of his vast epic, *The Dynasts*, which

---

*Despite the fact that this book seeks to describe British attitudes towards Napoleon, it seems relevant and interesting to quote the words of a distinguished Bengali, writing in elegant English. N.C. Chaudhuri (*Autobiography of an Unknown Indian*, London, Picador, 1999) expresses the rather surprising view that 'if any whole-hearted Bonapartists were to be found anywhere in the world at the end of the nineteenth century and the beginning of the twentieth, they were to be found in Bengal'. He goes on to claim that 'all educated Bengalis literally adored Napoleon and, not

took five years to write and which attempts the ambitious task of telling the tale, in prose and verse, of the Napoleonic Wars as they affected Europe and especially Britain; the second because *Napoleon, The Last Phase*, a study of Napoleon at St Helena and his treatment there, is the work of one who became Prime Minister in the 1890s and was a confirmed, though not uncritical, admirer of the 'Corsican ogre'. A very rich man, he was also an ardent collector of Napoleona, including the Emperor's travelling library and the cushion on which his head rested in death.

Hardy completed *The Dynasts* in 1908. It consists of 1,470 lines of prose, 7,931 of blank verse, 1,152 of rhymed verse, making 10,553 in all, not counting the stage directions and 'dumb-shows' – descriptions of huge mimes which add several thousand more lines to the work. The idea behind it predates its beginnings by many years. As a boy, Hardy had found in a cupboard copies of a periodical called *A History of the Wars* (i.e. the Napoleonic Wars) to which his grandfather, himself a military volunteer, had subscribed at the time. According to Hardy's second wife's *Early Life of Thomas Hardy*, these magazines, 'with their melodramatic prints of serried ranks, crossed bayonets, huge knapsacks and dead bodies, were the

satisfied with mere worship, tried to understand his military campaigns . . . although we regarded Napoleon almost as a god, and as invincible and unconquerable by straightforward methods of warfare, sometimes ascribing his defeat at Waterloo to the bribing of Grouchy, we still came to think of Wellington as the greatest general that ever lived'. Chaudhuri tries to explain this contradiction by saying that 'when we were thinking of Napoleon we had in mind only transcendental and supra-rational military genius, whereas we judged Wellington as the best rational and human general'. The young Chaudhuri, in other words, seems to have placed Napoleon on an unattainably high pedestal, where he assumed divine characteristics.

first to set him on the train of ideas that led to *The Trumpet Major* and *The Dynasts*.[†]

This is the fascination attaching to Hardy. He was, in time, only one remove from the Napoleonic period, and extraordinarily sensitive to the recollections and stories of those earlier times which enlivened his youth. Born in 1840, he never knew his grandfather, the collector of *A History of the Wars*, but he grew up knowing, and listening to, Dorset men and women who remembered those wars. In the preface to *The Trumpet Major*, he writes of the 'casual relics of the circumstances amidst which the action [of the novel] moves – our preparations for defence against the threatened invasion of England by Bonaparte'; and he goes on to describe the nature of those relics – such as an outhouse door punctured by bullet holes caused by someone using it as a target for firelock practice 'when the landing was hourly suspected'. This, he says, brought back 'to my imagination in early childhood the state of affairs at the date of the war more vividly than volumes of history could have done'.[1]

These memories and associations, a link with the past which was not so distant or indistinct as to dissolve into mere myth, remained with Hardy and grew, in his mind, to a resolve to encompass, in some form or another, the whole vast subject, to attempt 'an Iliad of Europe from 1789 to 1815', as he described it in a notebook in June 1875.[2] As the years passed, he continued to play with the idea, envisaging first a series of ballads, then a drama to be called, perhaps, *Napoleon* or *Josephine*. By 1886 he was thinking of Napoleon represented 'as

---

[†]Florence Hardy's two-volume life of her husband, *Early Life* and *Later Years*, published in 1928 and 1930, was in fact the work of Hardy himself. He carefully wrote in the third person and then destroyed his sources. (*The Older Hardy*, by Robert Gittings, London, Heinemann, 1978, pp. 180–81).

haunted by an Evil Genius or Familiar', and ten years later, while visiting Brussels and the field of Waterloo, he drew up the draft of a title page:

> Europe in throes
> Three parts, five acts each
> Characters: Burke, Pitt, Napoleon, George III, Wellington,
> And many others.

Hardy's bold, even bewildering, concept was not only to tell the story of an era in chronological detail, but to interpolate into that story the quasi-mystical comments of 'Spectral Figures', symbolising the powers that move the world. Hardy described them, in the preface to *The Dynasts*, as 'super-natural spectators of the terrestrial action, certain impersonated Abstractions or Intelligences, called Spirits', and they are divided into different categories: The Spirit of the Years, The Spirit of the Pities, The Spirit of Rumour, The Spirit Ironic, The Spirit Sinister. These spirits sometimes speak in chorus form, comparable to the interventions of the chorus in classical Greek drama. They do not make very easy reading for the modern consumer, who might feel tempted to echo what The Chorus of the Years exclaims at one point: 'We comprehend him not.' But Hardy's overarching view of history, his belief that events, great or small, are driven inexorably forward by 'automation or impulsion', that the actual actors in the drama – Napoleon, Pitt, Nelson – are puppets, blind expressions of the Immanent Will, is a recurring theme in *The Dynasts,* inseparable from the whole.

Hardy's own views about Napoleon are hard to define. He makes the Spirit Sinister say, as Napoleon threatens invasion of England, 'my argument is that War makes rattling good history; but Peace is poor reading. So I back Bonaparte for the reason that he will give pleasure to posterity.' But this comment is instantly rejected by The Spirit of the Pities: 'Gross hypocrite!' For the most part Hardy gives his real-life characters – Pitt, Castlereagh, Napoleon himself – lines to speak which reflect their known views and attitudes. Thus, in the debate in the House of Commons in April 1815, after Napoleon's escape from Elba (Part III, Scene V), Castlereagh describes him as:

> this man, who calls himself most impiously The Emperor of France, by Grace of God has, in the scale of human character, dropped down so low, that he has set at naught all pledges, stipulations, guarantees and stepped upon the only pedestal on which he cares to stand – his lawless will.

In the same debate, Whitbread, speaking on behalf of the Bonapartist Whigs, castigates the Declaration of Vienna – which defined Napoleon as 'an enemy and a disturber of the tranquillity of the world' and thus liable 'to public vengeance' – as 'abhorrent and our country's character defaced by our subscription to its terms'. These are poetic distillations of what was actually said in the debate: Hardy based himself on the Hansard record.

When it comes to Napoleon's innermost thoughts, Hardy resorts to imaginative invention – or possibly he had read or been made aware of the outpourings of the Longwood apologists; his reading list[3] contained several works in French about Napoleon though not O'Meara, Montholon, Gourgaud or Las Cases. Thus, Napoleon, depicted wandering about in a wood after the defeat of Waterloo (Act VII, Scene XI), wishes he had been killed earlier, in which case:

> My greatness would have stood, I should have scored
> a vast repute, scarce paralleled in time.

And yet, he goes on:

> . . . I found the crown of France in the mire
> and with the point of my prevailing sword
> I picked it up'.

As it is, he muses:

> I come too late in time
> to assume the prophet or the demi-god . . .

Great men are meteors that consume themselves
to light the earth. This is my burnt-out hour.

Possibly the best guide to Hardy's own feelings is found in the preface he wrote[4] for the French translation of *The Dynasts*. Here he claims that Napoleon is a particularly suitable subject for a playwright 'as a puppet of destiny; in fact he often regarded himself as such; and as such we may forgive him certain of his errors and ambitions, while waiting until in the future we can come to pardon him . . . if the *monist* theory of Causes and Effects . . . as the propulsive force that moved the personages is found to be the true theory of the universe'.

More interesting than this determinist view of history – that people act as they do because they are predestined to act thus, and so cannot be judged by any recognisable moral yardstick – is Hardy's treatment in *The Dynasts* of local, Dorset-based feelings about Napoleon. As may be expected, these are balanced between apprehension and hostility. An example of the first occurs in Act II, Scene V, set on Egdon Heath, where some locals, including militiamen, are waiting to fire the beacons which will give warning of Napoleonic invasion. One of the militiamen recalls how the whole of his eighty-strong company ran away, so dreadful were the stories they heard about Bonaparte. A woman fills in the details: 'they say he lives in human flesh and has rashers o' baby every morning for breakfast' (which is similar to what Thackeray's Indian servant told him; see p. 153).

As for hostility, Hardy describes a scene on the outskirts of Casterbridge (Dorchester), where a rough gallows has been built and an effigy of Napoleon hung on it. The time is after the escape from Elba and before Waterloo, i.e. eleven years later than the invasion scare. A local and somewhat simple-minded rustic arrives panting, fearful that he will be too late to see Napoleon burned. He thinks it really is Napoleon and is upset when bystanders explain that it is only an effigy. The vicar remonstrates that he, the rustic, cannot really image that 'we should be so inhuman in this Christian country as to burn a fellow-creature alive', to which the man replies, 'Faith, I won't say I didn't when we think what a blasphemous rascal he is, and there's not a more charnel-minded villain towards womenfolk in the whole world'.

These echoes of what Dorset folk were saying and thinking during the Napoleonic era found their way into Hardy's poem about his grandmother, his father's mother, possibly a model for Tess of the d'Urbervilles. She had been the subject of his very first poem, and in 1902, forty-five years after her death and during the period when *The Dynasts* was being composed, he returned to the subject, recalling her stories as he listened to them at the fireside in his youth:

> She told us of that far-back day, when they learnt astounded
> Of the death of the King of France,
> Of the Terror; and then of Bonaparte's unbounded
> Ambition and arrogance,
> Of how his threats woke warlike preparations
> Along the Southern strand
> And how each night brought tremors and trepidations
> Lest morning should see him land.

A case may be made, and with some plausibility, that here is the genuine voice of England, expressing its fears and hatred of the menace across the Channel, a voice at once more prevalent and popular than the doubts and scruples, however sincerely held, of the Holland House coteries, with their Bonapartist sympathies and their opposition to the war with France.

Archibald Philip Primrose, fifth Earl of Rosebery, is alleged to have said that he had three ambitions: to become Prime Minister, to win the Derby, and to marry an heiress. He strongly denied that he ever expressed such wishes. But he did in fact achieve all three: he was Prime Minister, a notably unsuccessful one, in 1894-5, in succession to Gladstone; his horses won the Derby three times; and he married Hannah, the enormously rich only child of Baron and Baroness Meyer de Rothschild. He was also the author of three biographies: of the first William Pitt, Lord Chatham, of Lord Randolph Churchill, and of Pitt the Younger. His fourth book, the second to be written after Pitt, cannot be called a biography because *Napoleon, the Last Phase*[5] deals only with the last years of its subject's life. But as a description of Napoleon's captivity at St Helena, as well as an attempt to place him in the framework of history, it is a readable and skilfully managed account of the years of exile. Its author describes it as 'an episode on which history has yet to record her final judgement'. That did not deter him from coming to a number of judgements himself, including the habitual unfavourable one of Sir Hudson Lowe.

Yet even here, the one-time Prime Minister – well read, sensitive, introspective and generally fair-minded – tempers his view with counter-balancing factors. Thus, he admits that after all the burdens and sacrifices imposed on the British people by twenty years of war, 'there was not the slightest hope of our government behaving with any sort of magnanimity [towards Napoleon]'. And he recognises that it was not Lowe, or Admiral Cockburn, who first had charge of Napoleon, who were responsible for the 'sordid and brutal policy' applied to the captive, but the government in London, of which Bathurst is the minister for whom Rosebery reserves his greatest contempt.[‡]

‡Bathurst also comes in for some harsh words from Charles Greville, the diarist and man about town, who as a young man had served Bathurst as private secretary. Writing after Bathurst's death in 1834, he says that 'his conduct to Napoleon justly incurred odium, for although he was only one of many, he was the Minister through whom the orders of the government passed, and he suffered the principal share of the reproach which was thrown upon the Cabinet for their rude and barbarous treatment of the

He repeats all the usual charges against Lowe – 'a narrow, ignorant, irritable man, without a vestige of tact or sympathy' – but at the same time allows that it was 'his luckless fate . . . to accept a position in which it was difficult to be successful, but impossible for him'. Like the Duke of Wellington, Rosebery charges Lowe with the inexpiable crime of not being 'what we should call, in the best sense, a gentleman'. But he recognises that Lowe, at the end of his career, was badly treated by the government.

Rosebery's analysis of Napoleon's personality and record is full of unanswered questions. What were his objectives, was he always sane, was he to some degree a charlatan, was he a lucky fatalist? The philosopher, Rosebery says – he appears to be casting himself in the role – will judge that Napoleon was launched into the world 'as a great natural or supernatural force, as a scourge or scavenger, to effect a vast operation, partly positive but mainly negative . . .' The scavenging consisted of clearing up the mess left by the French Revolution, the scourging was the Napoleonic challenge to the old monarchies, compelling them to set their houses in order. No one, Rosebery thinks, can question Napoleon's military greatness or his achievements as an administrator and legislator. But in the end, 'supreme power destroyed the balance of his judgement and common sense', which is not to say he was mad, but that his state of mind ceased to have any relation to, or control over, his ambition. The Napoleon of 1810 was not the Napoleon of 1801; 'he had obviously lost the balance of his reason'. Finally, Rosebery asks whether Napoleon was a great man, and answers that if greatness consists of natural power, 'something human beyond humanity', then he was certainly great. 'No name represents so completely and conspicuously dominion,

Emperor at St Helena' (*The Greville Memoirs*, ed. Lytton Strachey and Roger Fulford, 8 vols, London, Macmillan, 1938, vol. III, p. 65).

splendour and catastrophe . . . he was wrecked by the extra-vagance of his own genius.'

The book was published in 1900. This meant that Rosebery was able to study and compare most of the St Helena literature (with the exception of Bertrand's journal which, written in code, was not publicly available until 1949). He thinks little of the veracity of the various sources. Las Cases' accounts, where uncorroborated elsewhere, are 'wholly untrustworthy'. O'Meara's two-volume *Voice from St Helena,* the most popular of all the Longwood outpourings, is 'worthless despite its liveliness'. Antommarchi's book is not only worthless, but mendacious as well; Montholon's is declared of little value 'where it bears on the general strategy of Longwood'.

Rosebery adopts an uncharacteristically biased view of Forsyth's three volumes, based on massive documentation, in defence of Sir Hudson Lowe. He admits that they benefit from this documentation, and also that they prove the bad faith of O'Meara. But as a defence of Lowe, he says, they are futile because they are unreadable. This is equivalent to arguing that commentaries on the epistles of St Paul (themselves often heavy going), or research into the background to the feudal system, are useless because they are so dull. This derogatory attitude on the part of someone who wanted to be taken seriously suggests that on the subject of Lowe, Rosebery, like so many others, had a closed mind, with no wish to have it prised open, whatever the credentials of the opener.

For all his reservations and carefully counter-weighted arguments, he must be classed – he would not presumably want it otherwise – among the ranks of the Bonapartists, even if he realises that Napoleon represents 'a great human problem' which will ever remain one. By the time he wrote *The Last Phase,* Rosebery himself, though widely admired and looked up to, was a has-been in politics – a career which, though he reached its apex, he always affected to despise. One historian[6] has gone so far as to suggest that in choosing to write about

Napoleon's last years in captivity, Rosebery was identifying himself with the fallen warrior: 'it is that solitary figure standing on the rock of St Helena and gazing over the sea of the setting sun of whom he reminds us . . . behind, the murmur of the great world, where he was once the hero, now lost to him for ever; before, the waste of lonely waters and the engulfing night.' Writing in 1909, the author was not to know that Rosebery, though his political light was irremediably dimmed, was to live on until 1929, by which time he had become, in his own words, 'an impatient and uncomfortable corpse'.[7] It seems a fair guess that Napoleon, even if not stricken by illness, would not have welcomed such an extension to his ordeal.

APPENDIX III

Longwood and an unusual French assessment

Queen Victoria's act of reconciliation in 1855 was followed up in 1858 by the formal transfer to French sovereignty of Longwood House, its surrounding three acres and a further thirty acres of the so-called Val Napoleon, where the Imperial remains had lain for nineteen years.* In the succeeding century Longwood, after falling into almost complete disrepair, underwent a series of restorations and, together with the site of the empty grave, was visited by a large number of passing travellers.

These included, in July 1880, the Empress Eugénie, widow of Napoleon III, on her way homeward from the Transvaal, where she had prayed at the spot where her only son, the Prince Imperial, had been mown down by Zulus; and, nearly seventy years later, by King George VI, his Queen and the two Princesses, en route in a battleship to South Africa. What caught these visitors' attention, according to a report in *The Times* (which devoted a 'light' leader to the subject), was not so much the Napoleonic past as the amusements of the present, represented by the spectacle of local boys careering down 'the

---

*The transfer was made, by decision of the Privy Council, presided over by Queen Victoria, on 7 May 1858 to the Emperor of the French (Napoleon III) and his heirs. The newborn Third Republic assumed ownership in 1871.

biggest banister-slide in the world', consisting of a rail running down the side of the 629 steps from the top of Signal Hill.

At the official government-to-government level, the original bitterness over the treatment of Bonaparte remains, if not forgotten, buried in the distant past. On the 150th anniversary of his death, in May 1971, the joint Anglo-French celebrations at St Helena included a glowing tribute from the Governor, Sir Dermod Murphy, who declared 'the man in the street knows, and we are reminded by our education, that we are celebrating the memory of greatness, genius and courage'.

This display of goodwill has not always – in fact rather rarely – been echoed by French historians, who for almost two centuries have tended to vie with each other in castigating the British government in general and Hudson Lowe in particular for their conduct towards the defeated Emperor. But there are exceptions, and a notable one was M. Jean Duhamel, a prolific historian, specialising in studies of British institutions and modes of thought.[†] In his *The Fifty Days, Napoleon in England*[1] he gives a relatively balanced account of the story, nevermore so than in his closing pages, writing:

> Certainly with the passage of time, the judgements which successive generations have passed on the treatment of the Emperor at St Helena have been more and more severe. One can see, and that more clearly nowadays, what the attitude of the victors should have been. But after the trials they had endured, how could one expect them not to adopt an implacable attitude? The war, with its great loss of life, had lasted twenty years; the dead of Waterloo has just been buried. On the whole, English public opinion leaned against showing pity or pardon and saw nothing repulsive in the act of retaliation . . . in London Lady Holland's views did not gain acceptance.

[†]A barrister, he was also a member of the English Bar.

References and Notes

Chapter 1: ' ... The Hospitality of the British People'

1 The original is in the Royal Library at Windsor
2 *Napoleon surrenders*, by Gilbert Martineau, first published in France under the title *Napoléon se rend aux Anglais* Hachette, 1969, English translation John Murray, 1971, p. 42
3 *Napoleon after Waterloo*, by M.J. Thornton, Stanford University Press, 1968, p. 7
4 *Mémoires de la Reine Hortense*, Paris, Plon, 1927
5 Henri Carnot, *Mémoires sur Carnot*, quoted by Martineau, op. cit., p. 46
6 Louis Marchand, *Mémoires*, Paris, Plon, 1955
7 Marchand, op.cit.
8 F. Maitland, *Narrative of the surrender of Bonaparte*, and of his Residence on board HMS *Bellerophon*, London, Henry Colburn, 1826
9 Count de Las Cases, *Mémoriale de Ste Hélène*, Paris, 1823
10 *Charles James Fox*, by L.G. Mitchell, London, OUP, 1992, p.167
11 Mitchell, op. cit., p. 166
12 C.J. Fox, *Correspondence*, vol. VI, p. 349
13 Lady Holland, quoted in *The House of the Hollands*, by Lord Ilchester, London, John Murray, 1937, pp. 185–6
14 *Lord Granville Leveson Gower*, by Lady Granville, London, 1916, vol. I, p. 353
15 Mitchell, op. cit., p.175
16 Ilchester, op. cit., p. 188
17 *The First Napoleon, Documents from the Bowood Papers*, ed. The Earl of Kerry, London, Constable, 1925, vol. I, pp. 80–105
18 *Memoirs of Napoleon*, by M. de Bourrienne, London, Richard Bentley, 1836, vol. IV, pp. 22–35

19 *The Contemporary View of Napoleon*, by F.J. McCunn, London, Bell, 1914, p. 157
20 Bourrienne, op. cit., vol. III, pp. 82–3
21 *Napoleon's Death, an Inquest*, by Major-General Frank Richardson, London, William Kimber, 1974, p. 62
22 George Home, *Memoirs of an Aristocrat*, London, 1838
23 Maitland, op. cit., p. 210
24 Published in *Notes and Queries*, 25 April and 16 May 1908
25 Home, op. cit., pp. 239–41
26 *Correspondence and Table-Talk*, 2 vols, London, 1876, vol. I, p. 288
27 Appendix II to *Napoleon and His Followers*, ed. Clement Shorter, London, Cassell, 1908
28 *History of The Times*, London, 1935, vol. I, pp. 158 and 215–16
29 *Recollections of a Long Life*, by Henry Hobhouse (Lord Broughton), London, John Murray, 1909, vol. I, p. 323
30 Maitland, op. cit., p. 197
31 Maitland, op. cit., Preface, pp v–vi
32 *Bonapartism*, OUP, 1908, p.7
33 *Cambridge Modern History*, vol. IX, p.770

Chapter 2: A Helping Hand from Holland House

1   *Holland House*, by Leslie Mitchell, London, Duckworth, 1980, p. 17
2   *Thomas Babington Macaulay*, by J.L. Clive, London, 1973
3   S. Keppel, *Sovereign Lady*, London, 1974, p. 249
4   Mitchell, op. cit., p. 251
5   Mitchell, op. cit., p.253
6   Mitchell, op. cit., p. 258
7   Holland, *Foreign Reminiscences*, London 1850, Longman
8   But see p. 72
9   Gourgaud, *Journal*, English translation John Lane, London, 1932, p. 58
10 *Walter Scott, His Life and Personality*, by Hesketh Pearson, London, Methuen, 1954, pp. 126–7
11 Holland, op. cit., p. 205
12 Holland, op. cit., p. 310
13 Quoted in *The Napoleonists*, by Tangye Lean, London, OUP p. 197
14 In January–February 1998, an exhibition was mounted at Fountainebleau, with the title of *Books for Exile*, which included some of the books from the Elba and St Helena libraries

15 Holland, op. cit., p. 198
16 Holland, op. cit., p. 308
17 Holland, op. cit., p. 307. Holland claims he supplied the information, after talking to Louis Bonaparte (nephew)

Chapter 3: St Helena: The Gaoler and the Gaoled

1   One of the first English families he met were the Skeltons. He was Lieutenant-Governor of the island, and Longwood, where Napoleon was to be housed, was their official summer residence. Mrs Skelton greeted him there in October 1816. When the Skeltons left the following year, Napoleon gave Mrs Skelton a Sèvres cup.
2   *Monthly Review*, January 1900
3   Thiers, *Histoire du Consulat et de l'Empire*, 20 vols, Brussels, 1864, vol. 20, pp. 480–81
4   *Conversations with Wellington*, Earl Stanhope, OUP 1938, p. 327
5   Castlereagh, the British representative, at the 1814 negotiations disapproved of leaving him with the imperial title
6   Forsyth, *History of the Captivity of Napoleon at St Helena*, 3 vols, London, John Murray, 1853, vol. 1, pp. 58–62
7   Forsyth, op. cit., vol. 1, pp. 134–5
8   A Diary at St Helena, The Journal of Lady Malcolm, London, 1899, p. 19
9   This description of Longwood is based on the account given in *Napoleon in Exile* by Norwood Young, London, Stanley Paul, 1915, vol. 1, pp. 127–43
10 *Recollections of Napoleon at St Helena*, London, 1844
11 Rosebery, *The Last Phase*, London, 1900, p. 76
12 Gourgaud's *Journal*, op. cit., pp. 12–13
13 Gourgaud, Ste Hélène, Journal inédit 1815–1818, Paris, Flamarion, 1899, 2 vols, entry for 11 January 1816
14 Forsyth, op. cit., vol. 1, p. 195
15 Malcolm, op. cit., pp. 55–65
16 Lowe papers, ADD MSS 20155
17 Forsyth, op. cit., vol. 1, pp. 301 ff
18 Forsyth, op. cit., vol. 1, pp. 303 ff
19 *Napoleon in Exile, a Voice from St Helena*, by Barry O'Meara, 2 vols, London, 1822, Simkin & Marshall, vol. 2, p. 99
20 Richardson, op. cit., p. 123
21 Forsyth, op. cit., vol. 111, pp. 314–15
22 Forsyth, op. cit., vol. 111, pp. 314–15
23 Forsyth, op. cit., vol. III, pp. 32–6

[24] Forsyth, op. cit., vol. III, pp. 160–61

[25] Article in the *Cornhill* magazine, January 1901, based on Bingham's papers

[26] Norwood Young, op.cit., vol. 2, pp. 51–2

[27] Quoted in Norwood Young, op. cit., vol. 2, pp. 152–4

[28] *The Corsican*, by R.M. Johnston, a collection of sayings and writings of Napoleon, Toronto, 1910, p. 498

[29] Malcolm, *Diary*, op. cit., p. 10

[30] Notably Norwood Young, op. cit, vol. 2, pp. 54–5

[31] Masson, *Autour de Ste Hélène*, vol. 3, p. 191

[32] Norwood Young, op. cit., vol. 2, p. 106

[33] See Appendix I for Lowe's efforts to refute O'Meara

[34] This account is based on Forsyth, op. cit. vol.III, pp. 242–5

Chapter 4: Death and Burial

[1] Holland, *Reminiscences*, op. cit., p. 191

[2] Holland, *Reminiscences*, op. cit., p. 191

[3] Holland, *Reminiscences*, op. cit., p. 191

[4] Richardson, op. cit., p. 136

[5] Richardson, op. cit., p. 152

[6] *Napoleon at St Helena, Memoirs of General Bertrand*, tr. by Frances Hume, London, Cassell, 1953, pp. 199–206 and 254

[7] Ibid., pp. 199–206 and 254

[8] Richardson, op. cit., p. 170

[9] Letter published in *North British Advertiser*, 2 August 1873, quoted by Norwood Young, op. cit., vol. II, pp. 133–4

[10] Rosebery, op. cit., p. 227

[11] *St Helena*, Octave Aubrey, London, Gollancz, 1937, p. 547

[12] *The Times*, 11 July 1821

[13] Bertrand, op. cit., p. 262

[14] *Letters of Captain Englebert Lutyens*, ed. Sir Lees Knowles, London, John Lane, The Bodley Head

[15] Lutyens, op. cit.

[16] *The Emperor's Last Island*, by Julie Blackburn, London, Secker & Warburg, 1991, p. 193

Chapter 5: Soul of Evil or Greatest Man?

[1] *Byron's Letters and Journals*, ed Rowland Prothero, John Murray, 1898–1904, 6 vols, vol 2, p. 323–4

[2] *Byron's Complete Poetical Works*, ed. Jerome McGann, Carendon Press, 1993, vol. 7, p. 1.

[3] *Byron's Letters and Journals*, op. cit., vol. 3, p. 65

[4] Quoted in Lean, op. cit. pp 82–3

5. Advanced by Professor Wilson Knight, in *Lord Byron's Marriage*, London, 1957, pp. 266–7

6 Quoted in Lean, op.cit., p. 205

7 *William Wordsworth, the early years*, by Mary Morman, OUP, 1957, p. 572

8 *The Letters of William and Dorothy Wordsworth*, ed. E. de Selincourt, Oxford, 1937, vol. II, p. 489

9 *The Statesmanship of Wordsworth*, by A.V. Dicey, 1917, Oxford

10 Morman, op. cit., vol. 2, p. 154

11 *Correspondence of Robert Southey with Caroline Bowles*, ed. E. Dowden, Dublin, 1881, p. 81. He married her, as his second wife, in 1839

12 Quoted in *Britain and the French Revolution*, ed. H.T. Dickinson, London, Macmillan, 1989, p. 243

13 Quoted in *Politics and the Poet*, by F.M. Todd, London, Methuen, 1957, p. 137

14 *Letters and Papers of W.M. Thackeray*, ed. Gordon Ray, 1945, OUP, vol. 2, footnote to p. 563

15 *English Thought in the Nineteenth Century*, by D.C. Somervell, London, Methuen, 1929, p.71

16 *Life of P.B. Shelley*, by T.J. Hogg, London, Routledge, 1906 p. 383

17 Quoted in *The Life of William Hazlitt*, by P.P. Howe, London, Martin Secker, 1922, p. 88

18 B.R. Haydon, *Autobiography and Memoirs*, ed. from his journals by Tom Taylor, 2 vols, London, Peter Davies, vol. 1, p. 279

19 *William Hazlitt*, by Augustine Birrell, London, Macmillan, 1901, p. 207

20 *Progress of a Ploughboy to a Seat in Parliament*, ed. William Reitzell, London, Faber & Faber, 1933, p. 81

21 *Cobbett's Political Register*, 16 April 1814

22 Cobbett, op. cit., 21 January 1815

23 Quoted in *William Blake*, by Michael Davis, London, Paul Elek, 1977, p. 142

24 *Complete Letters of Robert Burns*, Alloway Publishing, 1987, p. 437

25 *Godwin, Uncollected Writings 1785–1822*, ed. J. Marken & B.R. Pullin, 1968

26 *A Fantasy of Reason*, by D.B. Locke, London, Routledge and Keegan Paul, 1980, p.203

27 *Letters of Verax, the Lives of Edward and John Philips*, London, Longman, 1815

28 *The Godwins and the Shelleys*, by William Sinclair, London, Faber & Faber, 1989, p. 390

29 *A Sultry Month,* by Alethea Hayter, London, Faber & Faber, 1965, p. 90

30 Hayter, op. cit., p. 91

31 *The Diaries of Benjamin Haydon,* ed. John Joliffe, London, Hutchinson, 1990

32 Joliffe, op. cit., p. 13

33 Joliffe, op. cit., pp. 76–7

34 *Standing in the Sun, a Life of J.M.W. Turner,* by Anthony Bailey, London, Sinclair-Stevenson, 1997, p. 324

35 Quoted in *The Art of Caricature,* by Edward Lucie-Smith, London, Orbis Publishing, 1981, p. 68

36 Quoted in *The Early Comic Strip,* by David Kunzle, University of California Press, 1973, p. 381

37 *Napoleon at the Boulogne Camp,* by Fernand Nicolay, trans. Georgina Davis, London, Cassell, 1907, pp. 317-33

Chapter 6: Reburial and Reconciliation

1 Thiers also wrote in similar terms to Lord Clarendon, the Lord Privy Seal in Lord Melbourne's government, whom he knew and preferred to Palmerston, the Foreign Secretary

2 Guizot. *Mémoires de Mon Temps,* Paris, Michel Levy Frères, 1862, vol. V, pp. 106-18

3 *Life and Letters of the Fourth Earl of Clarendon,* by Sir Herbert Maxwell, London, Edward Arnold, 1913, vol. I, p. 204

4 *The Works of William Makepeace Thackeray, 1898–1899,* 13 vols, vol. VII, p. 663

5 *Letters of the Prince Consort,* 1831–1861 London, John Murray, 1938, p. 181

6 *Letters of the Prince Consort,* op. cit., p. 230

7 *Letters of Queen Victoria* John Murray, vol. 3, p. 117

8 *Letters of the Prince Consort,* op. cit.

9 Quoted in George III, by Christopher Hibbert, London, Viking, 1998, p. 321

10 *Letters of Queen Victoria,* op. cit., vol. 3, p. 139

11 *Le Maréchal Canrobert,* Germain Bapst, Paris, Plon, 1902, vol. II, pp. 528-31

Appendix I: What Happened to Sir Hudson Lowe

1 Scott did not think much of Las Cases' Memorial either: 'when it comes to impartiality, Las Cases is not to be ranked much above O'Meara'.

2 *Napoleon's Last Journey,* London, John Murray, 1976, p. 23

3 Forsyth, op. cit., vol. III, p. 317

4 Ibid., p. 318
5 Ibid., p. 326
6 Ibid., p. 329
7 Ibid., p. 326

Appendix II: Hardy and Rosebery: Two Approaches to Napoleon

1 Preface to *The Trumpet Major*, Wessex Edition, London, Macmillan, 1912, pp. VII–VIII
2 Introduction to *The Dynasts, Complete Poetical Works*, ed. Samuel Hynes, OUP vol. IV, p. XI
3 Appendix B of Hynes, vol. V
4 *La Revue Nouvelle*, Paris, ed. Charles du Bois, Jan–Feb issue, 1928
5 London, Arthur L. Humphreys, 1900
6 A.G. Gardiner, *Prophets, Priests and Kings*, London, Dent, 1909
7 *Rosebery*, by Robert Rhodes James, London, Weidenfeld & Nicolson, 1963, p. 463

Appendix III: Longwood and an Unusual French Assessment

1 First published in Paris in 1963 (Plon), English translation 1969 (Hart-Davis)

Select Bibliography

Abell, Mrs Betsy, *Recollections of Napoleon at St Helena*, (London 1848, John Murray)

Aubrey, Octave, *St Helena 1937*, (London, Gollancz)

Bapst, Germain, *Le Maréchal Canrobert*, (Paris, Plon, 1902)

Bertrand, Henri, Grand Marshal, *Memoirs*, Deciphered and annotated by Paul Fleuriot de Langle, translated by Frances Hume, (London, Cassell, 1953)

Blackburn, Julie, *The Emperor's Last Island*, (London 1991 Secker and Warburg)

de Bourrienne, Louis-Antoine, *Memoirs*, 6 vols., Paris & London 1831.

Chateaubriand, François-René, *Mémoires d' Outre-Tombe*, 6 vols, (Paris 1860, Dufort, Mulet et Boulanger)

Clive J.L, *Macaulay, The Shaping of the Historian*, (London, 1973, Secker and Warburg)

Creevey, Thomas, *The Creevey Papers*, ed. Sir Herbert Maxwell, 2 vols, (London 1904 John Murray)

De Candé, François de Candé-Montholon and René Maury, *Napoléon, l'enigme resolue*, (Paris 2000, Albin Michel)

Dickinson H.T, *Britain and the French Revolution*, (London, Macmillan 1989)

Doris, Michael, *William Blake*, (London, Paul Elek, 1977)

Duhamel, Jean, *The Fifty Days*, translated from the French by R.A. Hall, (London, Hart-Davis, 1969)

Forsyth, William, *History of the Captivity of Napoleon at St Helena*, 3 vols, (London 1853, John Murray)

Geyl, Pieter, *Napoleon, For and Against*, London, Cape, 1949

Greville, Charles, *Memoirs*, ed. Lytton Strachey and Roger Fulford, 8 vols, (London 1938, Macmillan)

Gourgaud, Gaspard, *Journal de Ste Hélène*, (Paris, Flamarion, 1899, 2 vols)

Guizot, François, *Mémoires de mon temps*, (Paris, Michel Levy Frères 1862)

Hayter, Alethea, *A Sultry Month*, (London, Faber & Faber 1965)

Haydon, Benjamin, *Diaries*, ed. John Joliffe, (London, Hutchinson, 1990)

Hobhouse, Henry (Lord Broughton), *Recollections of a Long Life*, (London, John Murray 1909, two vols.)

Hogg, T.J., *Life of P.B. Shelley*, (London Routledge 1906)

Holland, Henry Edward, 3rd Baron, *Foreign Reminiscences*, (London 1850, Longman)

Home, George, *Memoirs of an Aristocrat*, (London 1838, Whittaker)

Howe, P.P., *Life of William Hazlitt* (London, Secker, 1922)

Hynes, Samuel, (ed.) *Hardy's Complete Poetical Works* (OUP)

Ilchester, Lord, *The Home of the Hollands*, (London, John Murray, 1937)

James, Robert Rhodes, *Rosebery*, (1963, Weidenfeld and Nicolson).

Johnston, R.M, *The Corsican*, (Toronto, 1910)

Kerry, Earl of (ed.) *Documents from the Bowood Papers*, two vols, (London, Constable and Co, 1925)

Knight, Wilson, *Lord Byron's Marriage*, (London 1957)

Kunzle, David, *The Early Comic Strip*, (University of California Press 1973)

Laurie-Smith, Edward, *The Art of Caricature*, (London Orbis Publishing 1981)

Las Cases, Count Emmanuel de, *Mémoriale de St Hélène*, (Paris 1823)

Lean, Tangye, *The Napoleonists*, (OUP 1970)

Locke, D.B., *A Fantasy of Reason*, (London, Routledge & Keegan Paul 1980)

Lutyens, Englebert, *Letters*, ed. Sir Lees Knowles, (London, John Lane, the Bodley Head)

Maitland, Capt F.L., *The Narrative of the Surrender of Bonaparte and of his Residence on board* H.M.S. Bellerophon (London, Henry Colburn, 1826).

Malcolm, Lady, *A Diary of St Helena*, (London 1899, A.D. Innes)

Marchand, Louis, *Mémoires, Paris, Plon 1955*, (OUP 1992)

Martineau, Gilbert, *Napoleon Surrenders*, translated from the French by Frances Partridge, (London, John Murray, 1971)

Napoleon's Last Journey, Translated from the French by Frances Partridge, (London, John Murray, 1976)

    Napoleon's St Helena, translated from the French by Frances Partridge, (London, John Murray 1968)

Masson, Frédéric, *Napoléon à Ste Hélène*, (1912 Paris, Albin Michel)

Mitchell, L.G, Charles James Fox, (London OUP 1992)

McCunn, F.J., *The Contemporary View of Napoleon* (London 1914, Bell)

Mormon, Mary, *William Wordsworth, the early years*, (OUP 1957)

O'Meara, Barry, *Napoleon in Exile, A Voice from St Helena*, 2 vols, (London 1822, Simkin & Marshall)

Pearson, Hesketh, *Walter Scott, his Life and Personality*, (London 1954, Methuen)

Reitzel, William (ed.), *Progress of a Ploughboy to a Seat in Parliament* (London, Faber & Faber, 1933)

Richardson, Major-General Frank, *Napoleon's Death, An Inquest*, (London, William Kimber 1974)

Rosebery, *The Last Phase*, (London 1900, Arthur Humphreys)

Selincourt, E, de, *Letters of William and Dorothy Wordsworth*, (OUP 1937)

Sinclair, William, *The Godwins and the Shelleys*, (London, Faber & Faber 1989)

Scott, Walter, *Life of Napoleon Bonaparte*, 1827, 9 vols

Shorter, Clement, *Napoleon and his followers*, (London, Cassell, 1908)

Somervell, D.C, *English Thought in the 19th Century* (London Methuen 1929)

Stanhope, Philip Henry, Fifth Earl, *Conversations with the Duke of Wellington*, (London, Cassell, 1953)

Taylor, Tom (ed.), *Life of B.J.Haydon*, (London 1853, Longman, 2 vols)

The Times, History of, vol I

Thiers, Adolphe, *Histoire du Consulat et de l'Empire*, 20 vols, (1864, Brussels, Meline)

Thornton M.J., *Napoleon after Waterloo*, (1968 Stanford University Press)

Todd F.M., *Politics and the Poet*, (London Methuen 1957)

Young, Norwood, *Napoleon in Exile at St Helena*, two vols, (London, Stanley Paul, 1915)

Index

Index